CHILD OF THE JUNGLE

The True Story of a Girl
Caught Between Two Worlds

SABINE KUEGLER

virago

VIRAGO

First published in Great Britain in 2005 by Virago Press as *Jungle Child*
This edition published in 2012

5 7 9 10 8 6

Title of the original German edition: *Dschungelkind*
© 2005 Droemersche Verlagsanstalt Th. Knaur Nachf. GmbH & Co. KG,
Munich

The moral right of the author has been asserted.

A CIP catalogue record for this book
is available from the British Library.

ISBN 978-1-84408-887-4

Typeset in Baskerville by M Rules
Printed and bound in Great Britain by
Clays Ltd, St Ives plc

Papers used by Virago are from well-managed forests
and other responsible sources.

MIX
Paper from
responsible sources
FSC   FSC® C104740
www.fsc.org

Virago
An imprint of
Little, Brown Book Group
Carmelite House
50 Victoria Embankment
London EC4Y 0DZ

An Hachette UK Company
www.hachette.co.uk

www.virago.co.uk

*Dedicated in loving memory to Ohri, my Fayu brother.
And to my children, Sophia, Lawrence, Julian and Vanessa,
the pride and joy of my life.*

CONTENTS

PREFACE

Several years ago, I was asked if I would be interested in writing a book about my life. At the time, I wondered what could be so interesting about my story that anyone would take the time to read it.

I have seldom spoken about my childhood or where I came from. Instead I spent years struggling to conform to a culture and way of life that was foreign to me. And yet, although it may appear on the surface that I have managed well, I cannot seem to find the sense of belonging or peace of mind for which I yearn.

I am unhappy. Feeling lonely and lost, I live the life of a vagabond, moving from one place to the next. My hope is always that in a new place I will finally find happiness. But each time I am disappointed.

The years are passing; I am getting older. After fifteen years in the modern world, shouldn't I have adapted to this way of life? And yet the older I get, the more my past seems intent on making itself heard, getting louder with each passing year. Buried memories are beginning to resurface, and the question of who I am and where I belong is growing stronger.

I feel like I am not living but merely existing. I go about

my business doing what is required of me. Yet my mind is tormented by a burning desire I cannot explain, a feeling of homesickness for something lost.

I don't want to continue this way any more. I want to feel alive again, to wake up in the morning with meaning in my life.

So I have decided to tell my story – to take a journey into the past, with the hope of discovering who I really am and where I belong.

But most of all I want to still the turmoil in my mind, to find the inner peace I so crave.

I want to tell a story, the story of a girl from a world lost to time. Like all mythic stories, it involves hate and love, forgiveness and brutality, and in the end, the beauty of life. But this story is no myth; it is a true story, and it is mine.

CHILD
OF THE
JUNGLE

1

MY STORY

Germany, 1989. It is the beginning of October, and I am seventeen years old. The clothes I am wearing were given to me – dark, oversized trousers held in place by a brown belt, a striped pullover that hangs down almost to my knees, and ankle-high shoes that are causing me great discomfort. I have hardly ever worn real shoes before, so this is a new kind of pain for me. The jacket I am wearing looks like something from another generation – it's dark blue with a hood that falls over my eyes when I try to put it on.

I am shivering from the cold; the icy wind is biting into my ears and nose. My hands have gone numb. Having barely known the winter, I don't know how to dress properly and do not have on gloves or a vest or even a hat.

I am at the central train station in Hamburg. I gasp as a bitter wind whistles past, clasping me in its icy embrace. It is shortly past nine or maybe ten, I don't remember any more. Someone had dropped me off at the station with instructions about how to find the right train. So confusing, so many numbers involved. After some time, I find the right platform – number 14. Clenching my small bag tightly against me, I put down the suitcase containing the few possessions I was able to bring with me. I look at the ticket in my hand for the hundredth time, trying to memorize the number of the carriage. Terribly nervous, with all my senses on overload, I carefully watch the unfamiliar white faces swirling around me, ready to defend myself should anyone attack me. But no one seems to even notice me.

An announcement blares through the speakers, but before I can understand it, the message is swallowed by commotion around me. Wide-eyed, I watch the scenario unfolding in front of me.

Then, for the first time in my life, I come face to face with a real train. It comes rushing toward me so fast, I step back in fright. This train looks different from those I had seen in pictures. It doesn't even have a smoke-stack. Instead, it is big and ominous, like a long, white snake slithering out of a black hole.

When the train finally draws to a halt, people start pushing and shoving to get on. I hang back for a few seconds, motionless, forgetting the cold as I stare with a mixture of curiosity and fear at the sight in front of me. A number on the side of the carriage catches my eye. I compare it with the number on my ticket and realize they are not the same. I look to the left and then to the right. The train seems to go on for ever. Blindly, I turn and hurry to the end of the train. Suddenly, there is a whistle; I startle and frantically look around. A man in uniform is holding up a strange baton. I start to panic when I realize that this must have something to do with the train's departure. Jumping through the nearest door, I get aboard just in time. The train is all ready starting to move.

Standing still for a moment, I am unsure of what to do next. My heart is beating so quickly. I spot what seem to be doors connecting the carriages, so I set off toward the front of the train, making sure not to make eye contact with any of the passengers as I pass. I start sweating as I push my way forward; there seems to be no end to the line of carriages. Suddenly, I find myself in a carriage that looks nicer than the ones I had passed through earlier; it's the first-class carriage. I have reached the front of the train and still not found the right number. My eyes fill with tears.

At that moment, a man comes out of a compartment and notices me. I turn away quickly, but he still approaches me, asking if he can help. I glance at him; he looks to be in his thirties and is wearing a dark business suit. He has brown hair, and his eyes are a brilliant blue. I show him the ticket and ask if he knows where to find the carriage with this number.

A man in uniform comes walking down the aisle and joins us. When asked if he can help, he glances at my ticket and tells me in an offhand manner that I am on the wrong train. I feel the colour drain out of my face. Noticing my fear, the conductor quickly tries to calm me down by explaining that there are two trains going to the same destination. Struggling to contain overwhelming panic, I ask him what I should do. He instructs me to get off at the next stop and take the next incoming train on the same platform. After checking the ticket of the blue-eyed man next to me, the conductor says good-bye and moves on. Standing alone with this stranger on a dark train in a foreign country, I feel a wave of helplessness and vulnerability wash over me.

Wild fears of rape and murder shoot through my mind. All the terrifying stories I had heard, the dangers of this modern world suddenly seem much more real now. How can I protect myself? I have no bow and arrow or even a knife on me.

The man smiles at me and asks if I would like to join him in his compartment until the next station. I shake my head, saying that I would prefer to stand in the corridor. He tries again, explaining that I would be much more comfortable seated in a compartment. Now I am convinced he is dangerous and up to no good. I say no, pick up my suitcase and take refuge in the little corridor between the carriages. He follows, asking where I am from. Hamburg, I tell him, my voice shaking, silently praying that he goes away.

To my great relief, the train starts slowing down. I am standing at the exit door of the carriage, but when the train comes to a stop, I suddenly realize I don't know how to open the door. I panic – what do I have to do, push or pull? I rattle the door handle harder, but nothing happens. The stranger reaches past me and pulls a red lever, opening the door. A gust of bitter wind blows into my face. What a relief to see the platform in front of me. One step and I will be out of danger. I mutter a quick thanks and clamber outside. As the door closes behind me, I turn to catch the last glimpse of the stranger at the window of the departing train.

There is no one else on the platform. It looks deserted and dark apart from a few dim lights above me. I start to shiver again. I can hear my teeth chattering and find myself longing for the comforting heat of the rain forest. I do not know what city I am in or what I will do if the next train doesn't come. Will I freeze to death here?

After what seems like an eternity, the next train finally arrives. This time, I am relieved to find the right carriage. I get on and notice a rack in the corridor filled with suitcases. Though I am convinced that my luggage will be stolen since I cannot guard it from my seat, I leave it there. By now I simply don't care any more. My legs feel weak, my feet hurt and I am exhausted.

Sitting down, I look for a seat belt but cannot find one, so I check the seat next to me. None there either. I look around and notice that no one is wearing a seat belt. This strikes me as odd, but maybe it is the way things are done here. After all, this country is foreign to me, even if my passport says I belong here.

Still shivering, I settle down. The gentle movement of the train starts to calm me. I take my shoes off and tuck my feet up under me to warm them, pulling my jacket tight around me. I gaze out the window and notice the moon. It looks so small and dim, like a fading flower. My eyes fill with tears that run down my cold cheeks. Even the moon here is a stranger to me, so unlike the one I am accustomed to. The moon I know is proud, so full of life and strength that its brightness casts my shadow on the ground.

I wearily lay my head back and close my eyes. The train continues to pick up speed. In my mind, I leave this cold, dark place and flee back into the familiar. Blue, white and green colours drift past my mind's eye. I am flying back into the warmth. The sun is shining, and its rays are flying with me. They dance around me, wrapping my whole body in their welcoming embrace. Visions of green fields envelop me, followed by colourful towns full of people, and then deep, dark valleys with narrow rivers etched through them. I can see the dense vegetation of great forests rolling their way over land.

Then the sea, vast and shimmering, stretching out beyond the endless horizon. And finally my beloved jungle with proud, tall trees forming a beautiful emerald carpet as far as the eye can see. This is a sight I have seen many times but which never fails to fill me with awe. The mighty jungle of West Papua. The lost valley. My home.

2

THE LOST VALLEY

As a child, I dreamed of flying like a bird, gliding high over the trees, driven by the wind. And then one day, I did fly. It was in January of 1980 that we began a trip that would change my life for ever.

My family had been living for about a year at Danau Bira, a small jungle base in West Papua, Indonesia – the western half of the island of New Guinea. The capital city, Jayapura, was located on the coast, and the flights from there to the interior of the island were long and expensive. Several families had built this small settlement in the middle of the jungle and named it Danau Bira.

The adults in the group, who came from a variety of countries, were linguists, anthropologists, pilots, missionaries and support staff. For them, Danau Bira was a place to come together to work on projects in the jungle. For us children, Danau Bira was simply paradise. On a two-mile stretch of land facing a lake, there were a number of houses, a tiny airstrip, a small post office, a meeting house, a guesthouse and a very small school. We even had a generator that provided electricity for several hours a day. A narrow, stone-covered path ran through the entire settlement. Two tribes lived in the area around Danau Bira: the Dani and the Bauzi. By the time we arrived, they had all ready been in contact with the world outside the jungle for some time.

Our wooden house was situated on a little hill with a wonderful view of the lake. There we lived, cut off from Western civilization, in what seemed like an almost perfect world.

I had just turned seven, had short blond hair and blue eyes, and was thin as a rail. As the middle child of three siblings, I was the wildest – constantly on the go and blessed with a lively imagination.

My sister, Judith, two years older than me, was the quiet, withdrawn one. She preferred sitting in a tree and drawing to more active pursuits. My brother, Christian, two years younger than me, was my most loyal follower, my partner in crime and (at times) my sworn enemy. He had a good memory, which, unfortunately, was often a disadvantage for me because when we argued, Mama believed him over me. As for my parents, they had chosen to leave Germany and pursue this unusual life in order to work as linguists and missionaries with a recently discovered native tribe.

The previous year, my father had established contact with the Fayu, a tribe located in a territory that had only been known to the outside world through myths and rumours. Since the initial meeting, Papa had made repeated trips to the Fayu, who lived in a region that was known to some as 'The Lost Valley'. And on a January morning in 1980, the moment for us to join him arrived. On that day, Mama, my brother, sister and I left our home in Danau Bira to go meet this new tribe.

When I woke up that morning, it was all ready hot and sticky. The sun shone its rays down on us without mercy. There was not a single cloud in the sky, only a brilliant blue canvas from horizon to horizon. Even the birds had crawled into the bushes to escape the heat of the day. Only a few brave insects chirped their songs from hiding places in the thicket.

I was excited and had all ready packed my personal belongings in a backpack. The previous evening my mother had given us two detailed lists. One was labeled 'To Pack'; the other was labeled 'Not Allowed.' To this day, I have never met anyone who can come close to mastering the practicality of packing the way my mother has.

Mama went through our bags one more time. 'Sabine,' she asked, 'did you pack everything as we discussed?'

I looked at her with big, innocent eyes. 'But of course, Mama.'

'Well, let's see then,' she said, and I knew I was in trouble. With a sigh, I opened my backpack. Shaking her head, Mama pulled out two glass jars that contained my favourite spiders.

'But Mama,' I said in desperation, 'they need me; I am their mother.'

'Then they will have to find a new mother,' she said without pity.

Angrily, I muttered, 'But Judith also packed stuff she's not allowed to take.' Judith looked at me with the shock of betrayal. Mama's search of her bag revealed various sketchbooks and her new dress from Germany.

Minius, a young orphaned Dani whom we had taken into our family, helped my mother carry the bags outside, where several other Dani men waited to load them onto the canoe that was to transport us to the small airstrip. The way would have been too difficult on foot with all our luggage. I was wearing long trousers, a T-shirt and a jacket that Mama had instructed me to take, though I didn't understand why. After all, it was terribly hot outside. I couldn't imagine being cold in this place.

'Do you want to go with the first or second canoe?' Mama wanted to know. I decided on the first canoe and went outside, where Christian was waiting. Judith wanted to go with Mama in the second one.

We skipped down the stone path until we came to a little wooden bridge, where I noticed a brightly coloured lizard hiding underneath. Immediately, I dropped my backpack and went to catch him. Christian, who was ahead of me, ran back and said, 'Sabine, hurry up! Otherwise the boat will leave without us. You can't keep the lizard anyway.' I glanced back up at the house and noticed Mama's warning glance as she caught me just as I was depositing the lizard in my pocket. To this day, I don't understand how she always managed to know what I was thinking. Disappointed that I hadn't found a replacement for my spiders, I took the squirming lizard back out of my pocket and let him go. I climbed onto the bridge, picked up my stuff and ran after Christian.

A few yards later, the path met the dock, which consisted simply of boards extending over the water. We jumped into the canoe and sat on some crossed boards that served as seats. A Dani man started the outboard motor and we glided out onto the lake. The wind felt so cool and refreshing. I let my hand glide over the water, splashing my face and hair. We motored past a few more houses and docks, and then a longer stretch of impenetrable jungle. Finally, we came to an open area that looked like a long, wide path of grass – the air-strip. It ran from the top of a small hill down to the lake.

If a pilot didn't manage to get the aircraft into the air in time, you could end up taking an unscheduled bath.

We tied our canoe to the dock, jumped out of it and carried all we could to the small air-strip. As we arrived, the preparation for the flight was in full swing. The pilot was walking around the helicopter doing his preflight check. The Dani men kept watch for the wild boars and free-roaming chickens in the area, any of which could complicate the take-off.

Our baggage was quickly piled up on the grass close to the chopper, ready to be loaded. Excitedly, I looked at the helicopter and could hardly believe that we were about to fly in it. It was a Bell 47 model with a rounded windshield covering the entire front of the craft. On both sides there were small platforms to which the luggage would be latched. It looked to me like a heavily laden dragonfly.

The pilot turned to me and asked, 'Well, Sabine, are you ready for your new home?' I beamed at him and answered that I was well prepared and really excited.

'Do you have your jacket with you?' Again the jacket! I answered in the affirmative and asked why I would need it. He explained that during the flight, it could get very cold as we ascended.

Suddenly I heard Christian scream. As I turned, the sight that presented itself threw me into a fit of hysterical giggles. He had been trying to help the Dani men chase a pig off the landing strip, but in the process slipped into a large pile of pig droppings in which he was still lying and screaming.

I ran over to him and, holding my nose shut, danced around saying, 'Christian stinks like a pig now.'

'No I don't!' he replied angrily.

'Yes, you do, and because you're so stinky now, we have to tie you under the helicopter in order to take you with us.'

'No!' he screamed even louder. 'That isn't true.' And with that he grabbed a handful of pig dung and threw it at me. With a scream of anger, I threw myself on him. We wrestled in the dirt in the middle of the landing strip, surrounded by amused Dani men. At that moment, Mama and Judith came running up the path, having heard the shouting from afar. The pilot only grinned as Mama raced past him. Judith stood a safe distance away from us, looking at us contemptuously and melodramatically declaring, 'I always knew I didn't belong in this family!'

There we stood, covered head to toe with pig dung and starting to attract hoards of flies. Mama took us down to the lake, where we had to undress and wash ourselves under her strict supervision. She put the dirty clothes into a bag, and Minius brought us fresh clothing from our luggage. Judith stayed behind, recounting to a very amused pilot the creative tale of how she ended up as a part of this family even though she was actually a real princess.

Finally it was time, and the pilot told us to climb aboard. The only place to sit in the helicopter was on a single, long bench. Christian sat next to the pilot, who was checking his instruments once again. Next to him sat Judith, then Mama, and I was on the outside. With all the skills that I could muster, I begged Mama to let me have the outside seat. After a lengthy discussion with the pilot, she finally consented. In order to lighten the weight to allow for more luggage, the doors had been taken off the craft, and so I now sat next to empty space and had an almost free downward view.

An American mechanic strapped us in and then double-checked the straps. I had been ordered to put on my jacket before, and having rarely worn a jacket here, I felt like I was suffocating. The mechanic stepped away and gave the pilot a hand signal indicating all was clear. Suddenly, there was a loud noise, and the great propeller started to turn faster and faster. It caused such a strong downdraft that everything loose flew away. The excitement grew in me as I felt us slowly lift upward.

As we rose higher and higher, the front of the helicopter dipped forward, and we flew out over the lake until we reached the edge of the jungle. With a swift upturn, we skimmed over the tops of the massive trees, flying higher and higher. I caught my breath in awe as I looked out over one of the largest rain forests in the world, stretched out beneath us as far as the eye could see.

I was flying! Adrenaline rushed through me, along with an unbelievable sense of well-being. The trees beneath us seemed so close, I felt that I only had to stretch out my hand to touch them. Green, brown and orange mixed themselves into a lovely palette, stretching until it lost itself in the blue horizon. I held my breath and closed my eyes as I felt the cold air whipping over my body. I hadn't anticipated such an extreme temperature difference. The wind blew with such a force that I tightly gripped the seat belt, thinking that if I let go, the wind would come and just carry me away.

As I opened my eyes, I saw two beautiful white birds flying beneath us. The noise of the helicopter didn't seem to bother them at all. How nice it would be to stretch out one's arms and be able to fly like a bird.

After what only seemed like a few minutes to me but was probably more like an hour, I saw the village of Kordesi under us. As we flew over the small settlement, natives from the Dou tribe stood and waved up at us. The helicopter banked to the left and followed the flow of the river, a mixture of bright blue and muddy brown. We followed it for about half an hour until the river made a sharp curve, and we spotted a small clearing.

We were to land on nothing more than a small patch of grass and dirt. To the left of it were thatched huts that protruded sporadically from the canopy of the jungle's trees. On the right side was a new wooden house with an aluminium roof, which was surrounded by several large trees. I caught sight of dark figures running for the cover of the jungle. Only one figure remained. My father stood at the edge of the clearing and waved as the helicopter settled onto the ground. I felt a jolt. We had landed!

3

THE FIRST
ENCOUNTER

The pilot turned off the motor. It took a while for the propeller to slow down and stop. Then suddenly it was completely silent – no singing birds, no human voices, no engine noises. A few seconds later, a wave of heat hit me like a hammer, causing me to lose my breath for a moment. I scrambled to loosen the seat belt and take off my jacket. Full of curiosity, I peeked out of the cockpit, but there was no human or animal in sight.

At this moment, Papa came around the helicopter and lifted me out, kissed me and told me to wait at the edge of the clearing. My legs felt weak and rubbery. Next, Mama climbed out of the chopper. Judith, in her elegant manner, extended her hand to Papa. He kissed her and helped her down.

'Papa, you stink! You need a bath!' she exclaimed. Papa just laughed and picked up Christian.

'No Papa,' he said, 'you smell good, and I am glad we're here with you.'

'So there,' Papa replied. 'Finally, someone who is happy to see me.' Whereupon Mama diplomatically replied that she was also happy to see him but a bath really might be in order. Papa did look unusual. I had never seen him with a beard, and his hair was long and scraggly. He wore a sweat-soaked bandana around his neck and a large hat. Even on that first day, it was obvious to us that Papa felt alive in the jungle. He had found his home.

I followed Judith to the edge of the clearing as Christian trailed behind us. We stood and waited, not really knowing what to do. Then in a strange language, Papa called out toward the trees. We watched with eager anticipation, waiting for an answer.

Suddenly we saw several men cautiously step out of the jungle. They slowly came toward us in a swaying, almost slithering way, making no sound as they walked. My siblings and I edged toward each other. We had never seen such wild-looking people. They were taller than the Dani and Bauzi, dark skinned with curly dark hair and completely naked. Their heads were partially covered with black emu feathers that hung over their eyes. Long, thin bones protruded through the soft tissue at the base of the noses – two going vertically and one horizontally. Over each eyebrow there was a flat bone, held in place by a thin headband made of tree bark fibres. Each man carried a bow and arrow in one hand and a stone axe in the other.

The strangers surrounded us, slowly blocking us in. Staring at us with black, expressionless eyes, their faces appeared sinister and threatening. I felt Judith grasping my hand tighter while Christian hid behind us. Closer and closer they came. When one man reached out and grabbed my big sister's long hair, I felt her flinch and realized from her gasping breath that she was about to panic. Fearfully, I called out to Papa. Upon hearing my voice, the natives jumped back in amazement. Immediately Papa appeared from behind the helicopter. He again spoke to the men, using that strange language I had never heard before. Then he turned to us and explained that these were Fayu men from the clan of the Iyarike and that we had nothing to be afraid of. They were simply curious because they had never seen white children before. Then Papa took my hand and led me to an older warrior. He laid my hand on the hand of the Fayu and said, 'This is Chief Baou, who gave us permission to live here.'

Chief Baou suddenly bent down to my level, took my face in his hands, and brought it close to his own. It startled me because I thought he meant to kiss me on the mouth, but instead he pressed his sweaty forehead to mine and rubbed them together. Papa laughed when he saw my surprised expression. He explained that the Fayu rub foreheads with one another as a means of greeting, as a sign of peace. The Fayu then did the same with each of my siblings. For the rest of the day, we walked around with dirty, sweaty foreheads.

Then the men began touching our hair, rubbing the skin on our arms and faces, wondering if under the white there was dark skin after all. They started talking to one another, voices getting increasingly louder with excitement. Their enthusiasm was contagious, and our fear was replaced by a curiosity that matched theirs.

After several minutes, I pushed my way through the group and ran to the helicopter. Arriving there, I noticed several naked women standing at the edge of the trees, some holding small children in their arms. They didn't look as dangerous as the men, so I slowly approached them. But as I drew closer, the children started screaming and the women ran back into the dense jungle. I stared after them for a while, wondering if they would come back. When they didn't, I went back to the helicopter, where Papa was unloading our baggage. The warriors helped him carry everything to the house.

Our new home was situated in a small clearing, bordered by the jungle on one side and the river on the other. Because the river frequently overflowed its banks, the house was built on stilts. The entire building was wrapped in a green screen to keep out insects and other unwanted guests from the animal kingdom. This would have been a good idea if it had worked. Despite the screen, we consistently had uninvited nightly visitors. Throughout our years there, Mama got up every night to hunt for rats and insects. Her weapon of choice was a Fayu arrow, which she skillfully used as a spear. I still have visions in my head of my mother in her long nightgown, flashlight in one hand and arrow in the other, tiptoeing after her prey. The Fayu were most grateful for her efforts, as they got to eat whatever she caught for breakfast the next day. The interior of the house was divided into two large rooms – one for sleeping and the other for cooking, eating and living. Next to the bedroom was a small bathroom. There weren't any doors, only sheets attached to the ceiling. If a sheet was pulled back, it meant we could enter the room. If it hung down, it meant the room was occupied.

Among the few 'luxury items' that Papa brought were two plastic sinks – one for the bathroom, the other for the kitchen. Rainwater was collected in several metal drums and then funneled into the house, where it was used for drinking and cooking. This worked well unless there was a dry spell. Then we had to carry water from the river and boil it.

In the kitchen was a small kerosene stove with two burners. On the opposite side, Papa had nailed a couple of simple boards that were used as shelves for pots, pans, plates, cups, etc. The 'pantry' consisted of a few shelves where we stored our food.

At one end of the living space was a table with a short-wave radio. Every morning at exactly 8 am, we called the base at Danau Bira as a safety measure. If three days passed with no contact from us, they would send out the helicopter. The preciseness of the hour was a matter of practical limitations – we, as well as the people at the base, had to conserve battery power and could not leave the radio on all day.

The sleeping space was divided into two halves – one for my sister and me, the other for my parents and brother. The beds were made of long boards nailed together, with thin foam pads on top. Mosquito nets were fastened above the beds and tucked into our mattresses at night.

Papa had constructed our bed under the window. He probably thought this would be cooler for us, as the window was simply a screen with no glass pane. And it was cooler, especially when it rained. Because when it rains in the tropics, it comes down in buckets – very large buckets! Frequently we would wake up in the middle of the night, soaked to the skin. Then we would have to get up, put on dry clothes, and creep to the other half of the room to our parents' bed. They would then wake up in the morning with three kids in their bed instead of one.

The 'bathroom' contained a sink, a tiny slab of cement for bedtime foot washing and a toilet. Since drinking water was precious, we didn't use the rainwater for flushing. Instead, Papa placed a bucket of river water next to the toilet.

On that first day, as we were inspecting the house, Christian noticed a startling sight on the wall: huge black spiders, each of which spanned the size of a dinner plate. We stared at them with the wide-eyed fascination that only children have toward such creatures. Noticing our stillness, Papa saw the spiders and called out for us not to move while he ran and grabbed a *parang* (a long machete). He came back holding it and approached the spiders.

'No, Papa! I want to keep them!' I shouted in horror, but it was too late. With a blow to each, he smashed them against the wall.

'Oh, cool!' remarked Christian. 'Look, the legs are still moving!'

The others were repulsed by the sight, but I began sobbing because my collection had lost such magnificent specimens. Mama took us outside to watch the helicopter leave while Papa stayed in the house and cleaned the spider-smeared wall.

I quickly forgot the incident with the spiders, as there was so much to see and discover in this adventure-filled new world. After the sound of the helicopter faded, I looked around. There was the bright, cool river that flowed past; the widely scattered huts of the Fayu; the dark, dense jungle; and finally, our new house. There were also the Fayu men, who watched me with the same interest I felt toward them. I don't remember what went through my head at that moment, but it surely must have been something wonderful. How could such a fascinating environment, a breathtaking and exciting future filled with beauty and magic bring something evil with it? I felt at home there, felt like this was the life I was born for, a life without stress in the midst of nature, untouched by modern civilization, a life I still dream of to this day.

And while I stood there, my life began to change. I was not a white girl any more; instead I began a transformation that would one day bring forth a young woman who would become a Fayu from the clan of the Iyarike.

That evening as we laid in bed, Papa came in, and together we said a prayer that became our nightly tradition. It is a prayer I pray to this day with my own children. It has accompanied me throughout the years and still gives me a tremendous feeling of security.

He who dwells in the shelter of the Most High will rest in the shadow of the Almighty. I will say of the Lord, 'He is my refuge and my fortress, my God, in whom I trust.' Surely he will save you from the fowler's snare and from the deadly pestilence. He will cover you with his feathers, and under his wings you will find refuge; his faithfulness will be your shield and rampart. You will not fear the terror of night, nor the arrow that flies by day, nor the pestilence that stalks in the darkness, nor the plague that destroys at midday. A thousand may fall at your side, ten thousand at your right hand, but it will not come near you . . . no harm will befall you, no disaster will come near your tent. For he will command his angels concerning you to guard you in all your ways.
—Psalm 91: 1–7, 10–11

4

THE FAYU TRIBE

The first night passed quickly. I awoke the next morning and could see the tall trees at the edge of the jungle through the window over my bed. The mysterious morning songs of the birds captivated my attention, lending wings to my imagination as I lay under my mosquito net, contemplating the adventures this new day would hold.

Judith was still sleeping, and it was quiet throughout the house. After a short while, I got bored and jumped out of bed to see if my parents were awake yet. They were still sleeping, so I ventured out to the small porch between the front door and the stairs leading down to the ground. I stood, breathing in the atmosphere, trying to absorb as much of it as possible. To my left I saw the Klihi River and longed to go swimming. The heat was all ready oppressive, and it would not take long for the sun to shine at full strength, forcing even its most loyal friends into the shade. Directly in front of me trees grew in a scattered pattern out of the brown loam. Ten yards to the right, at the edge of the jungle, stood a second slit-rail house, which I later learned was intended for guests. But since we almost never had guests, it was always empty except when Minius was with us. A few yards farther down was another small hut that Papa used as an office. He would spend many hours there in the years to come, learning and analysing the Fayu language.

As I pondered my surroundings, the Fayu village slowly awakened. They noticed me with interest and soon came closer, watching every move I made. For the first time, I saw women and children gathered in groups at a safe distance. The children were naked, and some had markedly distended bellies. I later came to understand that this condition was due to parasitic worms in their intestinal tracts. A few of them had reddish/orange hair – a result of vitamin deficiency.

What interested me most, however, were the women. They were smaller than the men, yet they came across as quite masculine. They were also mostly naked, with the exception of a small covering made of bark that stretched across their pubic area, very much like our modern string bikini. For me, the most striking aspect of the Fayu women was their breasts. They hung far down, sometimes all the way to their belly buttons. I had never seen such a sight! I sincerely hoped that when I grew up, I would not have breasts like that. When I later voiced my concern to my mother, she calmed me with the explanation that they only looked like that because they did not wear bras.

Although I could not understand what the Fayu were saying, one thing was certain: I was their primary topic of conversation. Their language sounded like a mysterious singsong. I was delighted with the sound because I had never heard anything like it. I stood and watched, smiling, but no one smiled back. The familiar noises of my siblings finally drew me back into the house. Everyone was awake, having been woken by the noise the Fayu made in their excitement. Mama was all ready engaged in making coffee, while Papa was mumbling in frustration at the radio, which didn't seem to be working. His handyman talents were rather limited and today he tried his luck by randomly tapping the radio with a hammer. Suddenly and without warning, it started working. Proudly he came and sat down, taking the plate Mama gave him. And so began our first breakfast in our new home.

I don't quite remember how the rest of the day went. I only recall bits and pieces. But one clear memory that remains is of us kids playing in the river. We could not understand why the Fayu children did not join us, instead sitting against a tree or huddling close to their parents and never smiling or laughing. They seemed to be scared, but we didn't know of whom or what. Everything seemed so peaceful there. We used hand signals to try to convince them to join us, but they ran away or started screaming when we approached them. Finally, we gave up and just played among ourselves.

Those first few days went by in a blur. We got up with the sun and went to bed when darkness fell. In the mornings, we would eat breakfast together – usually oats mixed with water and powdered milk or Weetabix with powdered milk. On special occasions, Mama made pancakes. Of course, with the few ingredients we had, we added lots of cinnamon and sugar to make them taste somewhat less bland. Occasionally, we found small insects in our breakfast that had somehow eaten through the packaging. After a while, this stopped bothering us – after all, it wasn't as if there were many other options for food. Mama called it 'your extra helping of protein', and we believed her.

One morning shortly after our arrival, the Fayu brought us several huge eggs. They were king dove eggs. Papa had entered into a trade agreement with the tribes' people: if they brought us food or interesting items, we would trade them knives, fishing line or hooks. And so on this day, Papa had traded for six huge eggs. We were delighted at the change. Oatmeal and Weetabix can get monotonous after a while.

We all sat around the table, watching Mama heat up the oil over the small kerosene stove. She picked up one of the eggs, holding it in both hands because it was so large. Then she broke it over the frying pan, but instead of the long-awaited trickle of white and yellow, a small, completely formed bird poured out, fell into the oil, and began to fry. We immediately became nauseated at the sight, and any trace of hunger disappeared. My heart sank as I saw the small dove. How lovely it would have been to watch him hatch and add him to my collection of pets.

After that initial experience, it took a while until we could eat the eggs again with any great enthusiasm. From that day on Mama opened every egg outside the house. If an egg all ready had an embryo in it, she gave it to the Fayu, who ate it with great delight. They were highly amused at our squeamishness.

A few days later, as I was playing with Christian, I noticed a young boy. He had been watching us from a safe distance for several days, intently interested in everything we did. He seemed to be less fearful than the other children. I presumed he was about my age.

What caught my attention was what he held in his hand – a child-size bow and several arrows. I slowly approached him and was surprised when he didn't run away or start to cry. As I reached him, I tentatively stretched out my hand toward his bow. To my great delight, he immediately handed it over.

Christian noticed this and joined us. Together we examined this masterful piece of craftsmanship. After a while, I tried to return the bow and arrows to the boy, but he shook his head and pressed it back into my hands. Christian was the first to understand that he was giving it to me. I was overjoyed! Using hand signals, I told the boy he should wait there and I ran back into the house, dumping the contents of my backpack onto the bed. I had to find something just as wonderful to give in return. Among my treasures was a small red mirror that I had got on the coast in Jayapura. Satisfied with my choice, I raced back outside and handed it to the boy.

The reaction that followed came as a total surprise to us. When he saw himself in the mirror, he screamed and dropped it. We laughed, and Christian picked it up off the ground and showed his own reflection to the boy. Then he offered the mirror back to him. In the meantime, several Fayu had gathered to see what was happening.

The boy took the mirror back and cautiously began looking into it, his eyes growing bigger and bigger. He moved his head back and forth, made faces and touched his reflection with his fingers. Soon great excitement broke out among the assembled onlookers. Everyone wanted to see his or her reflection. Christian and I were highly amused by this spectacle. We couldn't imagine what it must be like to see your own face for the first time. But since seeing our reflection was nothing new to us, our attention soon turned to more interesting pursuits – namely, playing with my new bow and arrow.

After a while, the Fayu boy approached us again, proudly holding his new mirror like a trophy. He pointed at himself and said, 'Tuare'. I pointed at myself and said, 'Sabine'. He repeated my name effortlessly. Christian introduced himself in the same way, but Tuare wasn't able to pronounce his name. We later learned that the reason for this was that Fayu words always end in a vowel, an aspect of their tonal language. So my brother pointed at himself again and said, 'Babu'. This was a name he had been given while living in Nepal, where both he and I were born. Tuare easily repeated this name, and from that day forth, my brother was called Babu.

Tuare became my closest companion, my best friend and childhood confidante. To this day, he calls me his sister. Tuare's relationship with us encouraged the other children to lose their fear as well. Slowly they joined us: Bebe, Abusai, Ohri, Baree, Ailakokeri, Dihida, Isori and many more.

We quickly noticed that the Fayu children did not know any games. We didn't concern ourselves too much with why this was and simply taught them our games. Every day we went swimming with them and played hunt-the-crocodile. We also taught them hide-and-seek, football and any other game we could think of. In return, they taught us how to construct and use bows and arrows. They showed us which animals could and could not be eaten, which plants were poisonous and which were edible. Our education also included how to make a fire without matches and how to make a knife out of bamboo – skills that filled us with great pride. Tuare and the others taught us how to build small huts to protect ourselves from the frequent rain.

Our favourite pastime, however, was playing with bows and arrows. We pretended we were lost in the jungle and had to survive by ourselves, which actually wasn't that far-fetched. In our game of survival, we had to hunt animals and then start a fire with which to cook them. If Mama, a trained nurse, only knew the things we ate during this time, she would have had a heart attack. We ate everything from spiders to bugs to worms to tiny fish.

Over time, I began to learn how to survive in the jungle, coming to know both its dangers and treasures. I learned to respect the jungle and to master it as much as is possible for a human. A love for the beauty and power of the nature around me began to grow. In the weeks and months after our arrival, I became like Tuare – a child of the jungle.

5

WHERE EVERYTHING BEGAN

I'm often asked how it came to be that a little German girl ended up living with a completely unknown people in such an isolated part of the world. To answer that question, I have to go back – back to the time and place where the story begins.

My mother, Doris, decided her future when she was twelve years old. She attended a presentation given by a friend of Albert Schweitzer, the famous doctor and missionary. There she heard of his work in Africa. The presentation so inspired my mother that she decided to become a nurse with the intention of working in developing countries.

Sixteen years later, she met my father, Klaus Peter Kuegler. Although he was working with the German airline, Lufthansa, at the time, he shared her passion. After he left Lufthansa, they got married and together completed their studies in linguistics. A year after Judith's birth, they began their work.

Their first assignment was in Nepal. There they lived among a tribe called the Danuwar Rai in order to study their language and to assist them as a developing culture. In December of 1972, I was born, and two years later, in 1974, my mother gave birth to my younger brother Christian.

Our family lived in a yellow clay house in the middle of the village. Even the floor of the house was made out of compressed mud. It had only tiny windows, so we mostly slept on the adjoining wood balcony to escape the heat that built up in the house. The climate there was subtropical; the landscape a mixture of green forests and dry, stony plains. Close to the village there was a wide river in which we bathed each evening.

We didn't have a shower or even furniture in our house. Food was prepared on a kerosene stove and eaten sitting on a straw mat that covered the floor. We slept on air mattresses. I spent most of my time with my sister, Judith, who herded goats – as was typical for village girls her age. Since we had no toys, we and the other children played with what nature provided.

I don't have many memories from this time, but I do recall lying on the air mattress with my sister, covered by the blanket we shared. I remember gazing into the night sky with its countless, brightly shining stars. They seemed so near that I would reach out my hand in the certainty of touching them. They twinkled between my fingers as I waved my hand across the sky. And so we fell asleep, surrounded by an unspoiled nature, far away from the ever faster developing civilization.

My mother once told me the following story from our days in Nepal. Late one afternoon, I came running to her and called out breathlessly, 'Mama, Mama! I have seen God!' Mama was quite surprised and wanted to investigate.

I took her by the hand and tugged her after me out to our balcony. I pointed at the Himalaya mountains that majestically framed the nearby horizon. Mama smiled as she grasped what I had meant. A beautiful vista lay before our eyes. The sun was just setting. Its rays played among the snow-covered mountain peaks, giving them the appearance of pure gold. It is one of the most awe-inspiring displays of nature in the world. We stood there together and admired the glorious sight. As the last rays disappeared, I said, full of disappointment, 'Now God is gone.'

Several years passed before the day we received the news that we could no longer stay in Nepal. For unexplained political reasons, all foreign organizations had to leave the country within three months. This was quite a shock to my parents, as they had been prepared to live there for an extended period of time. Now suddenly, they were supposed to go back to Germany, a country their hearts had left behind some years before – a country that we children had never even seen. With heavy hearts they packed up the household and sorrowfully said good-bye to the Danuwar Rai, who had become our family. Mama told me later that within a week, out of sorrow, her hair started turning grey.

Our long trip back to Germany led us through Kathmandu, the bustling and colourful capital city. Even then it appeared that I knew this was no longer my world: I cried, wanted to go back to our clay hut, to my friends, to the goats and the stars. I didn't understand why we couldn't simply go back. I was three years old.

And so it was onward to Germany, into a culture to which we children couldn't relate. Mama told me later that as we arrived at the airport in Frankfurt, I asked in puzzlement, 'So where is Germany?'

'But Sabine,' Mama answered, 'we are *in* Germany!'

My disappointment was so profound that I broke down in tears. You see, we had occasionally received packages from Germany, and I was so looking forward to meeting this kind, generous person named Germany, who had sent us all the nice stuff. My parents had never explained to me who, or more accurately what, Germany was.

During our stay in this foreign 'homeland', my parents prepared themselves for a new task. After lengthy discussion, they picked Indonesia as their next assignment and waited for their work visas to come through. On 23 April, 1978, it was finally time to start the journey to our new life. Instead of the highest place in the world, we were going to the lowest. The journey was taking us from the towering Himalayas to the swamp of Irian Jaya, Indonesia – today known as West Papua.

6

THE DISCOVERY OF
THE FAYU

Whether by coincidence or divine fate, on exactly the
same day we left for Indonesia, an American named
John made a startling discovery deep in the jungle of West
Papua. He had been assigned to build a landing strip in the
territory of the Dou tribe, who lived in an area that bordered
completely unexplored territories. John had been there several times previously to examine possible sites. This took
careful consideration due to the swampy nature of the region.
He finally decided on the outlying village named Kordesi
and had just finished examining the last touches of the landing strip when suddenly, four wild-looking men stepped out of
the dense vegetation. They were completely naked and had
bones through their noses and on their foreheads. Their
bodies were draped in the skulls of dead animals and uniden-
tifiable bones. In their hands, they carried bows and arrows.
While the men's appearance was frightening, their eyes were
in fact wide with terror and their entire bodies trembled. This
was their first encounter with a white man.

There was great excitement among the Dou villagers. Some explained to John that the men came from a tribe with whom the Dou had been engaged in years of brutal warfare. Once the situation had quietened down, John was able to hear several of the strangers' words and wrote them down in phonetic script. As it turned out, the four warriors were on an expedition to discover what lay beyond the boundaries of their territory. I still believe that it was no accident that the warriors happened to appear on one of the rare days that John visited the jungle.

Upon John's return to Jayapura, he gave his notes to a linguist who was engaged in documenting the languages spoken on the island. The result of his analysis indicated that this was a completely new language, belonging to what must be an unknown tribe.

This finding was discussed a few months later at a meeting my father attended. He was asked if he was interested in leading an expedition to make contact with the tribe, to mark their exact territory, to analyse what language group they belonged to, and to count how many members belonged to this unknown tribe. Papa asked to receive all of the available information about them. In response, he was given a piece of paper on which John had written the warriors' few words along with the sentence, 'Two to three days travel to the west of the Dou.' That was the sum total of what was known. After discussing it with my mother, Papa decided to take on the journey of discovery. The adventurer in him had come alive.

Papa immediately began preparations. He assembled a team that included Herb, an American researcher, and a Dani man who could speak Indonesian as well as the Dou language. His language abilities would end up playing an important role later on.

They flew by helicopter to the Dou village of Polita, which wasn't far from Kordesi (see map on page 40). From there, they paddled upriver via canoe, working their way westward, as John's directions indicated. After days of searching, they returned empty-handed. They had found absolutely no sign of the Fayu. The Dou and the Kirikiri, whose territories they had crossed, were unable to help them in the quest. They knew nothing specific about the Fayu's location, for none had dared venture into this territory out of fear of being killed. Those who had had never returned.

It should be noted that tribes rarely wandered from their own territories. Tribal warfare was common; the members risked death if they left the safety of their territories. Additionally, the Fayu had a legendary reputation for brutality and skill in warfare. The fear of them was so great that people didn't even like to talk about them.

In the midst of their resounding lack of success, Papa and the team received some unexpected good news. A Dou told my father about a Fayu woman who had married a man from the Kirikiri tribe – a unique situation given that tribes only interacted in warfare. With new hope, the expedition set forth into the Kirikiri territory in search of the woman. They found her in a clearing by the side of the river. She had all ready heard that someone was looking for the Fayu and wondered why anyone was crazy or suicidal enough to do that.

The Fayu woman was friendly and willing to help. Papa pulled out his hand-drawn map to show her the territory he had all ready searched. After much back and forth, she managed to explain that he had gone up the wrong river. She directed him up the Rouffaer River and then west onto the Klihi River. Papa's team was not outfitted for such a lengthy expedition, so they decided to return to Jayapura first to make better preparations.

As happens so often, things didn't go as planned. As soon as he arrived back in the city, Papa came down with his first attack of malaria. It was so bad that doctors didn't know if he would survive. Papa spent a number of days in the hospital, fighting for his life. He recovered after several months, and in February of 1979, he began his second expedition. In the meantime, we had moved as a family to the jungle base in Danau Bira.

This time, Papa tried to prepare for every eventuality, with supplies including an outboard motor, shortwave radio, jungle hammocks (a hammock completely enclosed with mosquito netting) and enough food for a week.

The party and their equipment travelled by helicopter to Polita. An additional Dani man joined them this time; however, there was still a language problem. Should they succeed in finding the Fayu, no one among their party could communicate with them. Papa spoke English. Herb could translate that into the Indonesian language, and the Dani man from the first expedition could translate that into the Dou tongue. But they needed someone to translate from Dou to Fayu.

The team asked the Dou for advice on the matter and was told of a Fayu mother and son they had captured some years ago during one of their wars. As a result, the boy had grown up among the Dou. When the boy came of marrying age, the Dou refused to let him marry one of their own, since he came from the hated Fayu. And so the young man left the Dou tribe, never to return. According to rumours, he currently lived in a border territory near the Kirikiri. His name was Nakire.

The team traded for a canoe on which to mount their outboard motor. They packed their equipment and set off in search of Nakire, laying a course toward the Kirikiri and the area where Nakire was rumoured to live. They found him with surprising ease, as Nakire all ready knew someone was looking for him. Throughout the years, we were repeatedly amazed at how quickly information is disseminated in the jungle.

He warmly greeted the team and offered them shelter, as it was getting dark. Nakire's one-man hut was very dirty and rather run down, but at least they had a palm-leaf roof over their heads. As they sat around the campfire that evening, Papa asked Nakire whether he would be willing to act as guide and translator for the team. He readily agreed, and thus the convoluted language chain was complete. It was painfully unwieldy – English to Indonesian to Dou to Fayu – but at least communication was now possible. The next morning, the now five-member party started upriver.

Prior to leaving on this trip, Papa drew a map including all information from his first trip and what the locals told him of the region. Centered on Polita, the map was divided into small, numbered quadrants. As a precaution, he also left a copy at the base in Danau Bira. This way, he could relate his approximate location during his daily radio call back to base. A helicopter stood ready to pick them up in case of an emergency, and the pilot could use the map to aid in the search. This first map was similar to the one shown on the following page.

After several hours of travel upriver, Nakire became increasingly nervous. He anxiously scanned the tree line as the river narrowed. The jungle loomed overhead, and dense vegetation crowded the banks. Nakire suddenly pointed at something, but Papa could only see a few fallen tree trunks. 'What is it?' Papa asked and then waited as the question went through the many layers of translation.

'A warning sign that we are now entering Fayu land,'

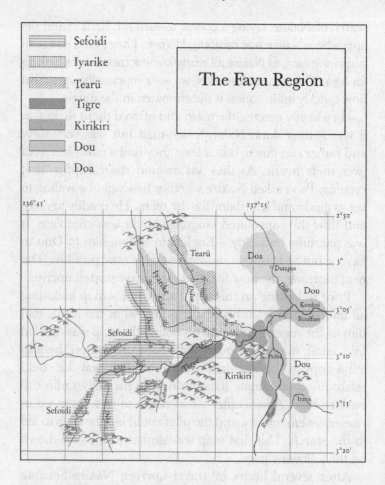

The Fayu Region

Sefoidi
Iyarike
Tearü
Tigre
Kirikiri
Dou
Doa

Nakire answered. It became quiet in the canoe. The only sounds came from the drone of the motor and the lapping of the water. Nakire jerked abruptly and whispered with fear, 'There! Can you see it?'

Papa carefully scanned the banks but detected nothing. Nakire told them that he saw eyes. Black eyes and dark figures. They were being followed.

Papa was later told that this was an established ambush spot. Anyone who came upriver was in danger of being shot. However, the warrior manning the station was so shocked to see a man with white skin that he didn't release the arrow.

They continued onward for several hours but couldn't find anyone. The few huts they saw were empty. Then they came upon several canoes lashed to the riverbank. *Where there are canoes, there must be people,* Papa thought to himself and decided to go ashore.

One of the Dani leapt ashore and tied the canoe to a tree. Papa told Nakire to get out next.

'No!' he said. 'You get out first!'

Confused, Papa countered that it made more sense for Nakire to go first. After all, as a Fayu, he could speak their language and clarify that they were coming in peace.

Not moving a muscle, Nakire only replied, 'I am too afraid.'

Papa didn't know at this time that the Fayu tribe was divided into several clans. The canoe was currently anchored in a border zone between the Iyarike, to whom Nakire belonged, and the Tigre clan.

Papa finally got out, followed by Herb and the other Dani. Their feet had barely touched the ground when they heard a noise behind them. Quickly, they turned around and froze. Standing in front of them was the scariest figure Papa had ever seen. The man's face radiated enmity. He carried a bow and arrow and was decorated with bones and feathers. His entire body was smeared with some indefinable substance that stank so horribly that Papa almost became sick.

Suddenly another man stepped into view from out of the thicket, with his bow drawn and aimed at Nakire. The arrow was outfitted with a tip specifically fashioned to kill humans. Quick as lightning, Nakire grabbed his own bow and pointed it at the man. No one moved or spoke for what seemed like an eternity. The hostility was physically palpable and it was hard to breathe.

Papa knew he had to defuse the situation quickly, so he leapt between the two and urgently raised an outstretched palm to each. 'Stop! Stop!' he called out, standing in the line of fire. 'We come in peace. Please put down your weapons.' As quickly as possible this was translated through the chain of languages. Meanwhile, Papa was looking death in the face, not daring to move. Finally, Nakire said something and lowered his bow. The tension dissolved as the Fayu lowered his bow as well.

The first Fayu who had come out, Ziau, was a leading warrior of the area in which the group had landed. Papa began to speak to him, repeating that he had come in peace and wanted to establish relations with the Fayu. The warrior signalled for Papa to follow him and lead the way into the jungle. Nakire stayed close to Papa, bow in one hand, arrow in the other. Just as Papa was about to step over a log, Nakire grabbed him and pulled him back. He pointed at the ground behind the log, where sharpened bone tips were camouflaged in the ground. Papa carefully stepped over the trap and kept going.

Finally they arrived at a small clearing. In the middle of it, there was a platform with a roof made of palm fronds. The odd stench grew stronger to the point that it was suffocating. The team pressed on anyway and approached the structure. Papa couldn't believe his eyes. What lay before him was a partially decomposed human corpse. It was bloated and covered with thousands of flies. Herb drew alongside my father and then froze in shock.

Ziau told them that a warrior from the same clan as Nakire had killed the man. Although the Fayu tradition demanded that revenge be exacted on that clan, he promised not to kill Nakire while he was under my father's protection. Additionally, Ziau offered to let the party stay the night, as evening was fast approaching.

As politely as he could, Papa thanked him and said that he would prefer to keep going. The party headed back to the canoe and breathed a sigh of relief (and stench-free air!). The team got back into the boat and was about to leave when Ziau suddenly reappeared. He called Papa over and told him something that probably saved all their lives. 'White man, go no further. Upriver they are waiting to kill you and your men.' When Papa heard this, his blood ran cold. He sincerely thanked the warrior and got back in the boat. They went back downriver in order to find a suitable campsite. It was getting darker, and the mosquitoes came out by the thousands. To cap it all off, large storm clouds gathered.

The team stopped at an abandoned hut they had passed earlier that day and set up camp. While this was happening, Papa radioed in their position. They were all afraid and didn't know if they were still being followed. Papa kept thinking about the figures Nakire had seen in this region earlier that day.

The hut was in disrepair, so the Dani men did their best to make it waterproof. In the event of further danger, they left most of the equipment in the canoe. It would make a quick getaway easier. The men unpacked what they needed for the night and made a campfire. The mood was rather sombre. No one was talking. They determined the order in which they would stand guard during the night, then Papa gathered them around the fire. Countless mosquitoes buzzed about.

Papa had many questions, the foremost being why there had been a corpse in the hut. Nakire provided this explanation: 'We keep our dead in our huts; sleep, eat and live next to them. As the corpse decomposes, we rub its fluid over our bodies. When it is deteriorated down to the bones, we take the skull and jaw and hang them up in our huts. When we move to another hut, we take them with us.'

When Papa again asked why, Nakire simply said, 'We Fayu have no hope ever to see our loved ones again, so we hang onto them as long as possible and keep the bones to remember them by.' Papa would not understand the full meaning of these words until much later.

It became dark. There was no moon or stars in the sky, so anything not illuminated by the fire was pitch black. A sudden crash of thunder and lightning ushered in the rain. Soon it was raining in torrents, and everyone fled into the hut, which, despite all efforts, was not watertight. Almost no one slept that night out of fear and discomfort. Papa was exhausted, completely disheartened and didn't know what to do. Should he break off the expedition? Should he keep going? Worn out, he eventually fell into a troubled sleep.

The newness of the next morning helped to restore Papa's spirits. The sun was shining again and promised a friendlier day. But appearances were deceiving. Herb woke my father with a worried expression on his face and dragged him down to the riverside. There, Papa saw the disaster. The canoe was completely filled with water; their equipment was gone, washed away by the storm. This unfortunately included the fuel reserves.

Papa's heart sank. This incident meant that they would have to cut their expedition short, failing for the second time. Thank God they had at least kept the shortwave radio with them.

As they sat around the morning campfire discussing what to do, one of the Dani men told them of a beautiful dream he had during the night. He had seen ten angels surrounding the entire camp with outstretched arms, each touching the other, creating a completely closed circle around the camp. A bright light surrounded them, illuminating the area and protecting the camp.

My father has always believed that God speaks in signs and dreams. On hearing the dream, he was filled once again with a sense of confidence. His faith and courage returned. Papa opened his Bible at random and began to read. Awe settled on him as he read a psalm that directly related to the situation at hand. The clear assurance that poured out of that scripture was the reason Papa later chose it as our daily prayer. It was Psalm 91.

Papa closed his eyes and breathed a prayer of gratitude. When he opened his eyes again, he found the team members watching him with anticipation. 'We go on,' he said.

They radioed in a request that the helicopter pilot deliver fuel and food. After giving a description of their location, they began clearing a landing pad. This took most of the day. By late afternoon, they had cleared enough space and started a large bonfire to serve as a beacon for the pilot.

It grew later and later, and still no helicopter came. The sun began to set. Nakire suddenly came to attention, stood up and looked to the sky. In a bit, the others could hear the faint drone of the approaching craft. The pilot had finally spotted the smoke. He landed and they quickly offloaded the supplies. It was important to hurry so that the pilot could get back to Danau Bira before nightfall.

The mood of this evening was in marked contrast to that of the night before. The men were relaxed and hopeful about what was to come. They spent the evening singing happily and discussing the continuation of the expedition. Guards were posted, but the night passed uneventfully. The next morning, they were better rested and full of anticipation.

The team started back upriver and passed the clearing where they had met Ziau. A few hours into the journey, Nakire suddenly refused to continue. Even Papa noticed it this time – a series of fallen tree trunks that signaled they were about to cross into a different clan's territory. Nakire was beginning to panic, so they pulled up onto a sandbank.

As the others prepared a midday meal, Nakire stood guard and nervously scanned the trees. Papa couldn't understand his anxiety, since Ziau had assured Nakire that nothing would happen to him as long as he was with the group. As they talked about this, Nakire explained that his anxiety had nothing to do with Ziau this time. Papa knew that the Fayu tribe was split into clans. Up to this point, he was aware of only three of them: the Iyarike, the Tigre and the Tearue. Now, much to Papa's surprise, Nakire said that there was a fourth clan.

'There is another group,' Nakire whispered. 'They are called the Sefoidi, and we are about to enter their territory. Please let us turn around. They are dangerous people. Not only do they kill anyone who enters their territory, they also eat them. Please don't continue.'

Cannibals, Papa thought, with a cold feeling in the pit of his stomach. *Now what do we do?* Papa distanced himself from the rest of the team, sitting by the river and praying about what he should do next. Then he remembered the Dani's dream and the Bible verse he had read that morning. Suddenly, he felt a surge of confidence fill his heart. He returned to the others, and after a group discussion they decided to keep going and together convinced Nakire to remain with them. They got back into the boat and continued on. A long time passed without them noticing any human activity.

The boat rounded a curve in the river, and suddenly a man came into view, sprinting along the bank in an effort to escape from them. Before he could reach a break in the dense underbrush, the boat came alongside him. The man stood frozen in terror. His whole body quivered as the team got out of the canoe and approached him. He tried to notch an arrow, but his hands were shaking too badly. He had clearly never seen white skin before.

Papa attempted to establish communication through his chain of translators, but without success. The man's fear overwhelmed his throat so that no words came out. Papa settled for asking him to pass along a message to his people, to let them know that the party had come in peace and would wait at this spot to meet with them. The man nodded quickly before running into the brush. The rest of the day passed, but no Sefoidi came.

Now what to do? The attempt at establishing contact had obviously failed. Papa knew the Sefoidi were in the area, watching them, but none was willing to show himself. The next day, the team decided to return and set up camp at a clearing back downriver that sat on the border of the territory between the Fayu and the other tribes (i.e. the Kirikiri, Dou and Doa). Before they departed for the clearing, they left several gifts in the hope that it would substantiate their claim that they came in peace.

A surprise was waiting for them at the clearing downriver. A large group of people was gathered there to give them a hero's welcome. It was an assembly of the Dou and Kirikiri tribes. Nakire's eyes widened in astonishment, as he had never seen such a large gathering of people. Papa couldn't

understand the commotion until one of his Dani compan-
ions proudly explained that no one had expected to see
them alive again. The team disembarked from the canoe
and was mobbed by the crowd. Everyone wanted to touch
them as though making sure the men's return wasn't simply
a dream.

As the team set up camp, Papa decided that they needed
to approach their quest in a different way. *If they won't let us
find them, we will simply wait here until they come to us.*

And then he practised patience . . .

7

INVITATION INTO THE STONE AGE

They waited for three days before their patience was rewarded. As they were eating breakfast on the morning of the third day, ten warriors suddenly stepped out of the jungle. They were fully armed and bore the decorations the team had come to associate with the Fayu. The warriors were led by Teau, one of the most dangerous war chiefs of the Iyarike clan. He gave off an air of distrust and hostility and immediately began rifling through the team's equipment. Simultaneously, his men surrounded the camp.

For three days, the warriors searched through every box, under every item, and in every pocket – all without saying a word. Papa told me later that he felt like he was going through immigration at an airport. But he knew that something important was happening, something that would affect everything. And so he let them search without protest.

On the third day, the searching stopped. Papa gathered his interpreters and asked Teau what he was looking for. Teau replied that two weeks before, Indonesian crocodile hunters had appeared in the Iyarike territory. They shot two of Teau's clan members, and now he was looking for revenge. Since the expedition's boat had an outboard motor, as did the crocodile hunters', he assumed that Papa was associated with them. That assumption led Teau to want to kill Papa. Had the warriors found a gun or crocodile skins, they would have slaughtered the entire team. However, since neither was found, Teau was forced to rethink his assumption about Papa's relationship to the hunters.

'What do you want, white man? Why have you come here?'

Papa replied, 'I am here because I am thinking about moving here with my family. I want to live among you and learn your language because I have an important message for you. A message of love and peace.'

Teau sat silently without moving, then looked up at Papa and said, 'White man, since you have arrived, hope has come into my heart. I'm tired of warring and killing. Please come back.' This astonishing reply caught my father completely off guard and almost moved him to tears. He asked Teau when he should return. Teau responded that Papa should come back to this clearing in three moons. 'That gives me time to tell my people that they should not kill you, that you come in peace.'

The two groups said good-bye. The warriors disappeared into the jungle as the team prepared to go back to Polita. Nakire decided to rejoin the clan of his birth and so left with the warriors. Papa returned to Danau Bira full of joy. He could hardly wait for the three months to pass.

Meanwhile, in the jungle, events were in motion that we only came to know much later. Teau may have decided to give up warring for the three months of waiting for the white man to return, but the majority of the Iyarike disagreed with him. Two groups formed. The smaller group, which included Nakire and Teau, believed that the white man would return. The larger group did not and thought that surely the white man was lying about having a message of love and peace. After all, no one had ever taken an interest in the Fayu before. Why should these people be trusted?

The group's discussions revealed the extent to which the Fayu had lived in isolation. 'Let us continue to make war and live as we always have. Haven't we always believed that there were no people outside of our territories? None of them have ever cared enough to help us or even contact us. Let us forget the white man. We don't need him.'

But Teau had sufficient influence that he and Nakire were able to convince the dissenting group to wait the three months. Then they would know if the white man would keep his word.

Exactly three months later, representatives from most of the Fayu clans assembled on the appointed day at the clearing, which would later be named Foida. They waited anxiously when suddenly there was a faint sound that grew louder and louder. They ran to the river-bank and watched as a long canoe came around the curve – motor in the back, white man in the front. The white man had kept his word! Nakire later told us that he cried with joy when he saw him.

As Papa and the team got out of the boat, he was met with curious and friendly gazes as well as astonishment. This was also a significant moment for two primary reasons. First, it established a level of credibility for Papa. Second, and as important, this event unified (even if for a brief time) the Fayu clans. The desire to see the storied white man with their own eyes overcame the civil war that existed among them.

White people had been to the Fayu land before, but none of the tribe members knew this. They were not even aware that a world existed beyond theirs, let alone white people. Even we only heard of this earlier encounter a few years ago, when a journalist called my father. He had read of a Dutch expedition in Irian Jaya in the 1940s that had made contact with the Fayu. This information had apparently not been passed on and had been forgotten by the tribe – an alarming trend that is typical of a dying culture.

Shortly after his arrival in Foida, Papa was visited by Chief Baou. A member of the Tigre clan, he was the oldest of all the Fayu chieftains and was known as the most dangerous and cold-blooded of all the Fayu warriors. Chief Baou wasn't a physically imposing man, but the people respectfully stepped aside and made room for him. Nakire whispered to Papa that this was the most respected of all the chieftains and that his word carried weight among all the clans.

Chief Baou was a quiet man who never smiled. We children always went out of our way to avoid him. Not so much because we were scared, but because everyone else did the same. He radiated a sense of authority that was almost tangible.

Papa respectfully greeted the chieftain, offering him something to eat as they sat around the campfire. Through the chain of interpreters, Papa started the conversation by saying that he hadn't come to rule but to serve them. He had no intention of contesting Chief Baou's authority, but rather was willing to submit to it. Papa then expressed his desire to bring his family to live among the Fayu. Papa asked directly, 'Chief Baou, do I have your permission to move here with my family?'

Chief Baou lowered his head and sat, immobile. Silence descended as the people waited for the chief's verdict. Several minutes passed before he looked up. 'Yes, white man. You have my permission. I want you and your family to come and live with us.'

You could hear the collective sigh of relief. Nakire grinned from ear to ear. (Papa later told me that this was one of the highlights of his life – 'though it couldn't compare with the moment of your birth,' he added with a wink.)

My father asked Chief Baou where he should build his house. 'Right here,' the chief replied, pointing to a spot on the ground. And so exactly there, Papa built our first house.

It is not for nothing that Chief Baou was known as a wise man. He considered problems from all angles. Although we didn't know it at the time, the clearing he chose for our house was a neutral zone between the clans. Chief Baou's decision assured that none of the clans could claim Papa as personal property. And in this way, it was guaranteed that conflict wouldn't break out over access to us.

In the months that followed, Papa spent a lot of time with the Fayu: to strengthen their trust in him, to learn their culture and language, and to build our house. He hired some Dani men to help with its construction.

In the process of the Dani helpers getting ready to leave for a resupply trip back to Danau Bira, one of them had left his machete laying on the ground outside. A Fayu warrior picked it up and happily strutted around with it. Papa could all ready hear the helicopter in the distance when the Dani man came to him and complained that the Fayu was refusing to return his machete. Papa went to him but got the same response, a *hau* ('no' in Fayu). Becoming increasingly frustrated, Papa tried to explain that the machete belonged to the Dani man who was about to leave. The Fayu man laughingly refused and said that if Papa wanted it that badly, he should take it from him. Now angry, Papa forced him to return the machete.

As soon as the helicopter was gone, the Fayu man went immediately to Papa and demanded a replacement machete. Papa was confused and knew that he had missed something. He called for Nakire, who had become his advisor on language and culture.

'Is it true that I have to give this guy a new machete?'

Nakire looked at him with a surprised expression. 'What? You haven't given him one yet?'

'Of course not!' Papa answered. 'It wasn't even his machete. Why should I give him a new one?'

So Nakire explained the Fayu 'law' of ownership. If someone leaves an object lying around unguarded, that clearly means he or she doesn't value that object, and whoever finds it is the new owner. And since Papa had forced the Fayu to give up his new piece of property, Papa was clearly obligated to provide a replacement.

So Papa gave in and presented the man with a new machete. This was the beginning of a long learning process. Each of us would have many of these learning opportunities as we adapted to their culture.

My father pushed through and eventually finished the house. And in January of 1980, the time had come for us to join him.

8

A DAY IN THE JUNGLE

Life in the jungle soon became normal for us. Like every other family in the world, we developed a daily routine. The sun was all ready up when I woke in the mornings. We would dress quickly, then our family would eat breakfast together and school lessons would begin. This was always pure torture for me, since outside the window there was a myriad of adventures waiting just for me. The birds and sun called out and seemed to tell me that I should come out and play. I could hear the sound of the river streaming past our house and the singsong voices of the Fayu.

Every now and then my Fayu friends would look in through the window and signal that they were ready to play. But Mama was very strict in this regard. I had to stay inside until all my schoolwork was completed to her satisfaction. Often, I would try to talk her out of this. 'Look at Bebe outside. He looks so sad. I think he needs me!'

'And your English lessons need you, too,' my mother would dryly respond. 'Bebe can do without you for another hour.'

Our schoolwork was part of an American curriculum that had been designed for children growing up outside the school system. During our stays in Danau Bira, our lessons would be corrected by a teacher. If no qualified teacher was available, one of the other missionaries filled in.

When I was about nine years old, the first real teachers came from the United States. They spent two years in Danau Bira in order to better educate us 'jungle children'. Today, I admire their courage and discipline. Especially in the beginning, they had a difficult time with our small group of a dozen half-feral children. But they eventually managed to establish a well-functioning and successful educational program. Whenever the children were in Danau Bira, they attended the tiny school there. The teachers corrected the work we had done while in the jungle and gave us new assignments to take back with us.

As a young child, I never did understand the point of going to school. This made dealing with difficult subjects all the more frustrating. What I hated most were the math problems. 'I just don't get this,' I murmured, angry yet again.

Christian, who was five years old, poked his head out from under a table, where he had been occupied with a spider. 'Sabine,' he squeaked. 'There are three of us kids, and if Mama gives us each three sweets, that's three times three, and that is nine.' His head disappeared back under the table.

'And where on earth would Mama get so many sweets?' I moodily replied.

Mama had heard everything from the room next door and was delighted with Christian's mathematical under-standing. So she asked him, 'Christian, if there are five birds on a branch and a hunter shoots one, how many are left?'

His head reappeared from under the table. 'None,' he promptly replied.

'And why is that?' Mama asked, astonished.

With a sigh, Christian replied, 'They would've all flown away because the hunter made so much noise with his gun.' His head disappeared again. Mama shook with laughter.

Christian really can give the coolest answers, I thought with some envy.

On the other hand, my attempts to deal with difficult questions never worked. When Mama once asked me what the capital city of England was, I suddenly had a very convincing fainting spell and fell off my chair onto the ground. Unimpressed by my theatrics, Mama emptied a glass of water on my head.

'If you don't start concentrating more, Sabine, you'll have to repeat the second grade,' she said, annoyed, while handing me a towel.

This opened up a whole new range of possibilities. 'Great idea!' I exclaimed. 'Then I don't have to study so hard next year.' Finally, it was my turn to leave Mama speechless.

What could school offer me anyway? I could all ready climb and shoot arrows better than most children could, with the obvious exception being my Fayu friends. I knew how to survive in the jungle, knew which animals and plants were edible and which were poisonous. Why on earth should I bother learning which general fought in which war and what 12 times 6 resulted in? My Fayu friends could only count to three anyway. The Fayu language only had words for 'one', 'two' and 'three'. The next numerical value after that was simply called 'a handful'. Two handfuls made ten, add in a foot for fifteen, and both feet to make it twenty. Surely nothing beyond that was necessary.

When I had to write an essay but didn't feel like it, I

would simply place random letters together. For quite a while, my American teacher thought that I was writing in German and gently encouraged me to write in English. One day, in frustration, the teacher came to my mother to ask for her help. Mama quickly set her straight that what I was writing did not remotely resemble German. For a while after that, I had nothing to laugh about . . .

I think that I worried my parents quite a bit during these years. 'She's not lacking in intelligence,' wrote my teacher. 'Sabine is simply lazy and refuses to concentrate.' These were the words that repeatedly graced my report cards. As a consequence, I was supervised more strictly and had to do my schoolwork alone at our table while Mama prepared lunch. This way, she could keep an eye on me.

Not that this helped a lot. While I was outwardly occupied with my schoolwork, my mind was busy outside, building a fire or swimming in the cool water of the river. As soon as I had completed the day's assignment, I would dash outside with my bow and arrow. My patient friends would be waiting to greet me with beaming smiles. We ran off and lost ourselves in the imagination of childhood. The rest of the day was spent playing and exploring, forgetting that there was a world beyond our own.

I didn't need shoes, a jacket or a raincoat. I was free, free like the sun whose rays shone through the trees, like the river that happily splashed along or the wind that drifted aimlessly about and the wonderful, cool earth beneath my toes. All these elements of nature made the jungle seem as alive to me as any person. It is difficult for me to convey the wonder of this time without it sounding exaggerated or overly poetic. But for me, the warm rain was my playmate, the cool wind my friend. And every evening the sunset painted the sky like a glorious display of fireworks: red, yellow, blue, purple – an array of colours that defy description.

At night, our family would sit around the table, under the comforting glow of the kerosene lamps. Thousands of miles from civilization, we played Scrabble, Uno, or Headache. Sometimes Papa would tell us stories about a rabbit named ZigZag. Because of his disobedience, this bunny became involved in a variety of misadventures, including being chased by an evil eagle. The moral of these stories was hard to miss, but we loved them anyway.

And at the end of a full day, with the warmth of the sun still caressing my skin, I would climb into bed, bow and arrow beside me. Papa would say the evening prayer with us. Then, to the accompaniment of thousands of insects and birds, I would fall asleep, tucked inside the mosquito net. Sweet memories of the day fuelled dreams of the adventures still awaiting me.

9

NIGHTLY VISITORS

After only several months had passed, it all ready seemed as though we had always lived in the jungle. Time flew by, and I forgot what day it was or even what month. My activities were determined by the course of the sun. When the sun rose at 6 am, I got up; when it was directly over me, I ate lunch; and when it set at 6 pm, it was time to go to bed.

The nights for us kids were usually undisturbed, but not necessarily for Mama, who was occupied by hunting critters. Sometimes she woke up Christian, who in the meantime had become quite proficient with a bow and arrow. I, on the other hand, she made sure not to awaken because I was (as Judith liked to complain) a walking orphanage for animals. I collected everything that swam, crawled or flew.

Yet one night, a commotion woke me up anyway. The largest rat I had ever seen had laid claim to our food. It attacked the beam from the flashlight with such ferocity that even I, who loved all creatures, did not want to add it to my collection. Christian was about to stab it with an arrow when it jumped at the weapon. This startled us so much that we went screaming in all directions.

The noise woke up Papa, who immediately took command of the situation. Despite the rat's ferocity and generally bad attitude, I begged him to spare its life, and Papa grudgingly agreed. He tried at first to simply chase the rat out of the house. This was not successful. So it turned out to be a long and lively night whose victorious end we celebrated with tea and biscuits.

But rats weren't our only visitors. Cockroaches, spiders and all manner of vermin enjoyed the hospitality of the house and the food stored within. Mama was quite perplexed as to why they continued to multiply despite her best efforts to put food beyond their reach. Among the measures she took was mandatory sweeping three times a day. Then one day, Mama discovered the problem.

It was once again my turn to sweep. I remembered Papa's technique of sweeping the crumbs and debris through the cracks in the floor rather than out the door. That seemed practical to me, and so once I had swept it all into a pile, I chose the largest gap and happily made the mess disappear through it.

In a shocked voice, Mama said, 'Sabine! What are you doing? No wonder we have so many pests in the house. You should be old enough to know better. How did you come up with such an idea?' Angrily, she shook her head.

I really should have known better. Netting was stapled to the bottom of the floorboards, so the crumbs collected themselves in what became a lovely dining room for all the insects. But I had the best of all excuses. 'But Mama,' I replied, 'that's how Papa does it!'

'Sabine is right,' Christian added, in defense of the truth.

'Papa always does it that way when you're not here.' Papa began to whistle, feigning innocence from the back room.

'Now really, Klaus Peter, what were you thinking . . .' Mama began to rant.

'Oh, Doris,' he tried to calm her. 'What are a few more pests? They're our only visitors anyway.' He winked at us kids, and we started to laugh. Mama just looked at him. I don't think that was the end of that conversation because from that day forward, we all employed the proper technique.

A few days later, Papa woke up in the middle of the night with the feeling that something was wrong. He got out of bed, flashlight in hand, and checked to see if everything was all right with us kids. For a time, he stood by our beds, trying to figure out what had woken him up. Then he noticed that everything was quiet. No chirping insects. No ribbiting frogs. Then he heard a splashing sound.

Upon looking out the front window, Papa noticed, aided by the brightness of the moon, that the river was full to the edge of its banks, though it hadn't even rained. We later realized that there had been a storm in the mountains at the river's source.

Papa's first concern was the boat that was anchored to the shore with nothing but a simple wooden stake. The stake was no longer standing upright but shaking back and forth from the boat being pulled at by the current. Our only transportation! Our only lifeline! The boat must be rescued at any cost, since we had recently been told that the helicopter was temporarily grounded. In the case of an emergency, the boat was now our only way out.

Papa hurried toward the front door. Suddenly he saw in the beam of his flashlight that a huge snake was blocking his path to the door. He froze. The snake hissed and raised itself to attack position. Papa looked around in desperation. What should he do? The machete was behind the snake on a shelf next to the door. Papa thought for a moment and decided to crawl over the table. From there he should be able to reach the machete. Without taking his eyes off the snake, Papa slowly got up onto the table and crept forward. The snake followed his every move. Eventually, he reached the shelf and grabbed the machete. Now, how was he going to get close enough to the snake to kill it?

He turned the flashlight off and waited for a split second. Pointing it at the snake's last location, Papa turned it back on while raising the machete in the other hand. The light blinded the snake for a few crucial seconds, and Papa used the opportunity to slash at its head. That didn't kill it, so the two of them fought for a while. When the snake was finally dead, Papa picked it up with the machete and carried it outside and slung it into the river. At precisely this moment, the stake worked itself loose, and the boat started floating downriver. Desperation propelled Papa into the water, and he barely managed to grab the rope and pull the boat back to shore.

To this day, Mama likes telling this story in great detail. How Papa crawled over the table with raised flashlight, his hair wild about his head, shorts hanging off his hips. She had been watching the whole thing from the doorway of the bedroom.

The next morning at breakfast, we children delightedly listened as Papa regaled us with tales of his exciting night. The dishes were used as props, the coffee spoon serving in the role of the snake.

'Papa,' I said with disappointment, 'why didn't you wake me up? I could have helped.'

'Me too, me too!' Christian cried.

'That is very kind of you,' Papa answered. 'And while I know that Christian is good with a bow and arrow and that you, Sabine, are great at catching animals, I somehow felt better knowing that you were safely tucked under your mosquito nets. It is easier to protect you that way. Can you understand that?' Christian and I nodded together.

But it could happen again when Papa isn't in the house, I thought to myself. *And if then, by chance, the same thing should happen again, I'm sure we could manage by ourselves.*

Very pleased with myself and yet with a profound feeling of security, knowing that Papa would always protect me, I ran outside and jumped in the river for my morning bath.

10

THE FIRST WAR

It happened about three months after our arrival in the Fayu village of Foida. We had noticed that the children were sometimes afraid, but we didn't know why. Much to our delight, they had increasingly joined our games and seemed to enjoy themselves. Sometimes, though, they still appeared nervous. This was especially true when members of neighbouring Fayu clans came into the village.

On this particular day, the children were behaving as they did when we first arrived: they stopped playing and sat with their backs to a tree or near their parents. I suddenly noticed a whole group of Fayu I had never seen before. They arrived in two canoes. The unusual thing about this group was that it was comprised of only men.

I was sitting around a fire with Christian, Tuare and Bebe. We were eating *kwa* (breadfruit), which tastes something like a cross between nuts and potatoes. They grow on trees that are found scattered throughout the jungle. Kwa is dark green and covered with fat, soft spikes. To eat them, we would lay them in the fire until their skin blackened – a sign that they were ready.

Tuare took one out of the fire and squashed the still-smoking fruit with his bare foot. It was roughly the size of a honeydew melon, and the inside consisted of a white, stringy material, which contained walnut-size brown seeds. We picked out the seeds, peeled them, and ate them with great delight.

We had just eaten our second kwa when the canoes appeared. The natives around me became nervous. Tuare and Bebe quietly disappeared with the women and other children into the thick rain forest. Christian and I stayed seated at the fire; after all, it isn't every day that something so interesting occurs.

The Fayu men of our village grabbed the bows and arrows they always kept within arm's reach. They assembled as the canoes landed and the unknown warriors stepped out. We watched them with the innocent curiosity of children. Wild and dark, they were dressed in full regalia. Their stark gazes passed over us. No one smiled or rubbed our foreheads in greeting. I was a little unnerved by their failure to display this customary courtesy. There was something different about this situation.

Papa came out of the house to greet the newcomers. He gave them some fishing line and hooks as a welcoming present and tried to engage them in conversation with the bit of Fayu he had learned. The first hour went by quietly.

Christian and I grew bored with the nonactivity and decided to go swimming. As we were splashing around in the water, the voices on shore became increasingly louder. I climbed up the small embankment to see what was happening. The Fayu were standing and sitting in two groups – the men of our village on one side, the strangers on the other. It was obvious they were arguing, and their hostile expressions indicated the gravity of the situation. Each of them held a bow in one hand and an arrow in the other. Always a bad sign.

Another hour passed as the atmosphere thickened with tension. Loud talk became aggressive shouting. At that point, Mama called for us to come into the house. We hurried, knowing something was very wrong. Papa followed us into the house, barring the door behind him. Christian and I climbed up onto the bench and watched out the window.

Now, all of the men were standing and facing each other. Their voices climbed into an upper register, screaming at each other. Suddenly the atmosphere changed again. I felt something I had never felt before. I can best describe it as dark, heavy and threatening. The sun was still shining brightly, but somehow it seemed darkness had descended.

As we were watching, individual men began stomping their feet. They moved in circular motions and began repeating a single word, *ooh-wa, ooh-wa, ooh-wa*. This was the war cry. Soon all had joined in the chanting. They faced each other, stomping the ground, arrows notched in their bows. Then they started to run in what seemed to be a predetermined choreography. First, the two groups would run away from each other until they were about fifty yards apart. Then, they ran at each other, stopping when only a few yards separated them. More stomping would ensue, and then the war dance would be repeated.

They kept this up for hours without seeming to tire. During this time an odd thing occurred. It was almost as though the warriors entered a trance state: eyes glazed over, and movements became stiff and robotic. Their voices changed, some becoming quite deep while others grew shrill. *Ooh-wa, ooh-wa, ooh-wa*, for hours.

After a while, I got bored and grabbed a book I had been reading. I had almost finished it when I heard a scream of pain that pierced the chanting. Then another one . . . the war had begun.

Everything moved quickly, as though time speeded up. Mama and Papa made us stay away from the windows to avoid the stray arrows that could easily have pierced the screen. Thank God this never happened.

After a while, silence descended. The visiting Fayu carried their wounded to the canoes and paddled away. Papa was the first one out of the house, wanting to help where he could. After a few minutes, he called out that everything was safe. We all went outside, except for Judith, who was still too scared. The scene that awaited us was not pretty; several men bled from arrow wounds. The entire village was dull-eyed, and no one spoke a word. To our relief, there were no fatalities. Mama began to bandage the wounded; Papa and I helped her.

From this point on, it became common practice for the warriors to come to our house following a battle so that Mama could dress their wounds. In tropical climates, wounds can get infected within a few hours if left untreated. And so prior to our arrival, many warriors died from infection in the days following a battle even though their wounds were superficial.

Chief Baou was not among the wounded this time. He sat apart from the other warriors and stared at the ground. Papa stood in front of him, unable to find the words to express the storm of emotions that flooded through him. He turned away and shepherded us into the house. The darkness of night descended on the village.

We had now experienced for ourselves the Fayu reality of war. This time it was the Sefoidi, who lived far upriver, and the Tigre, one of two clans whose territory bordered our house. But it could well have been any combination of the clans. How many times must this have happened before? A tribe that once numbered in the thousands had been reduced to mere hundreds by their civil war.

This would not be the last conflict that occurred around our house. But it was the first and last time I witnessed the battle escalate to this degree. Looking back on it now, I don't remember ever fearing for my own safety during any of the conflicts that raged about the house. Perhaps it was due to my firm faith that God and Papa would keep me safe. I also felt hope for the Fayu that the future held something brighter for them.

As I lay in my bed that night, serenaded by an orchestra of frogs and insects, I offered my own little prayer – a prayer from the heart of a child. *Dear God, please give the Fayu peace.*

11

ANIMAL COLLECTION,
PART ONE

Children everywhere develop their own hobbies, and even in the jungle, I found mine. One day, Mama came into the kitchen and saw me loading up the table with pots and pans, bottles of oil, towels, our good kitchen knives, and so forth. Astonished, she asked, 'Sabine, what are you doing?'

With sparkling eyes I bubbled, 'I need this stuff! Outside is a Fayu who wants to trade me a baby crocodile. In exchange, he's getting all of this,' indicating the loot on the table with a generous gesture.

'And where is this crocodile supposed to live?' Mama cautiously asked.

Without hesitation I replied, 'In the bucket. I've all ready filled it with water.'

Mother turned around and walked out onto the landing where the Fayu was waiting. She sent him home with the words, 'This trade won't be happening.' Then she came back inside and explained a few rules of the house:

1. One always asks permission first.
2. One does not trade away items that do not belong to you. (I protested that since my name was Kuegler, too, I had a claim to the items. Mama responded by asking if I had ever even used the cooking pot.)
3. It is difficult to raise a crocodile in a bucket.
4. One should try to see it from the animal's perspective. Imagine how lonely the little crocodile would be without his mother and siblings.

I viewed all of Mama's points with suspicion, sure that they were aimed at depriving me of my heart's desire. But her final argument finally convinced me.

As I grew older, my love for animals increased and I became a passionate collector. Sadly, this didn't always end well. My curiosity caused the death of quite a few of the poor little creatures. I grieved deeply over all of the animals that left me through the years, either through death or escape. 'They all go to heaven,' Mama explained to me. And so I imagined heaven to be a place where hundreds of animals ran around, waiting to become my playmates.

All of my animals got names, down to the smallest spider. The mouse was named George, the parrot was Bobby and my spider was called Daddy Longlegs. The cassowaries were named Hanni and Nanni; then there was Jumper the tree kangaroo, Wooly the cuscus and on and on it went.

I collected spiders along with their eggs and put them in large jars filled with dirt, grass and wood so they would feel at home. Then I would catch small insects with which to feed them. But I could never understand why the spider eggs never hatched. In my learned estimation, they had everything they needed. I carefully observed them in their natural habitat and so knew exactly what kind of home to make for them. Then one day, I happened to walk into the bedroom and saw, to my horror, Mama spraying insect spray onto the eggs. I let loose a bloodcurdling scream and charged, intent on saving my babies. But it was too late.

'Mama, how can you be so cruel?' I sobbed.

Mother gave a deep sigh. 'Look around you. Don't you think you have enough animals?'

I looked around. Hanni and Nanni were standing behind me. Bobby was squawking in the window, and George was running around in his box. On a small shelf stood various containers with spiders, bugs and frogs. My cat, Timmy, was asleep on the bed, and Wooly sat on a bar watching us. I looked at Mama in confusion and answered, 'No.'

Mama groaned, and then we reached a compromise. She would no longer touch my collection, and in exchange, I would keep them outside. She was tired of constantly chasing spiders and frogs around the room. That same day Papa built me a few shelves behind the house where I could keep my beloved collection.

Of all the animals, Timmy the cat was clearly my favourite. He had been given to me in Danau Bira. Timmy was a magnificent white and black tomcat, secure in his own superiority. When we brought him with us to Foida, the Fayu were quite confused. They had never seen a cat before and asked if he was a dog, or maybe a baby boar. Papa said he wasn't either of those. 'Well, what is it then?' they wanted to know.

Papa didn't know how to respond, since they had no word for it, so he answered, 'That is Timmy.' So from that day forward, 'Timmy' became the Fayu word for 'cat'.

To demonstrate Timmy's abilities, Papa tossed him into the air several times. Each time he landed on his feet. The Fayu were amazed and nodded approvingly. Several hours later, a few of them came to Papa and sadly reported, 'Our dingoes (hunting dogs) cannot do that. They keep landing on their backs and yowling.'

The dingoes had obviously not seen a cat before, either. Shortly after Timmy's arrival in Foida, one of them tried to steal a rat Timmy had killed. With a convincing hiss, Timmy charged and raked the dingo across the nose with such force that it ran off, yelping the entire length of the village. From that day forward, Timmy was the king of the jungle. All of the dingoes gave him a wide berth out of their great respect for those claws.

Timmy became quite the jungle cat. Every evening at precisely 6 pm, he would disappear into the jungle to hunt. He would reappear at exactly 4 am and stand at the door, begging to be let in. We couldn't ignore him – he just got louder and louder. Papa would always say that he didn't need a watch any more. Timmy was more reliable than anything Timex could turn out. After we let him in, Timmy would jump into bed with me and lay across my neck, back feet on one side of my head, front feet on the other. This had been his favourite spot since he was a kitten.

One day I generously allowed Timmy to sleep with Judith, since he loved wrapping himself in her long hair. But the following morning, there was great wailing and gnashing of teeth. Timmy had chewed off a large chunk of Judith's hair at the top of her head. The sad remnants poked up in all directions like a bad cowlick. I couldn't help finding it hilarious, and I collapsed into hysterics.

Mother grabbed me by the collar and marched me out of the house. 'You can only come back in when you've quieted down. We don't laugh at other people's pain, no matter how funny it looks.'

After a short while outside, it occurred to me that I hadn't eaten breakfast yet. I put my hand over my mouth to try to mask my giggles and went back inside. Mama greeted me with a warning look. She had given Judith a big straw hat to wear to cover up the damage. At the sight of this, I lost control of my giggles again and ran back outside to calm down. On my next careful attempt to approach the breakfast table, I unfortunately glanced at Papa, who was sitting with his head lowered, shoulders quaking. I got stitches in my stomach from laughing so hard. Mama kicked me out again but at least gave me breakfast to take with me this time. By evening, Judith had calmed down and could laugh with me, but her bed was off limits to Timmy from that point on.

The hunting dingoes also captured my interest. I always wondered why they never barked but only howled. Later I found out that they aren't really dogs but a kind of Asian wolf. The Fayu treated them like their children. They gave them much time and attention in order to train them as hunting dogs. Whoever had a well-trained dingo also had meat. I tried several times over the years to tame a dingo into being my pet but never succeeded. They were simply too wild to snuggle up with.

The first time Papa saw a Fayu woman breast-feeding a dingo, he couldn't believe his eyes. But in the course of time, we got used to it and accepted it as normal. It was common practice for the women to breast-feed their children and a dingo puppy (or even a piglet!) at the same time. I assured Mama that once I had a baby, I would surely have enough milk to also breast-feed a puppy.

'Well, Sabine, at least you'll make the news, but concentrate on growing up first,' she replied.

For me, the rain forest was like a zoo except that the animals ran around freely. West Papua's jungle has no tigers or apes, so the largest animals we saw were cassowaries, wild boars and crocodiles. But the smaller animals were of greater interest to me anyway, since they were easier to catch. Whenever I 'discovered' a new species, I would run into the house to get a container for it. The only type I was never able to catch alive were snakes: it was dangerous to handle an unknown snake, as many of them were poisonous.

The Fayu quickly learned of my love for animals and figured out how to use this to their advantage. With my help, they were guaranteed a good trade, since I would wear down Papa with my begging until he traded something for the animal.

One day, a Fayu came to me with a large, dead snake. It had attacked a dingo between our house and the village, and so the native killed it. This particular snake had a wonderful red-brown colour. Its scales gleamed in the sunlight and felt like pure silk. I held it in my hands and mourned its death. Christian stood next to me, and we examined every inch of it.

As I glanced up, I noticed Judith coming out of the house. Unbidden, a plan formed in my mind. She was only a few yards away and hadn't noticed the snake in my hands. Christian started grinning when he saw my expression; it was one he knew well. I grabbed the snake by its tail and swung it like a lasso over my head, releasing it in Judith's direction. Much to my surprise, my aim was better than I thought it would be. The snake flew through the air and wrapped itself around her neck. That my sister didn't drop dead of a heart attack is a miracle in itself. That she still speaks to me today is an even bigger one.

Spiders were high on my list of favourites. I would spend hours watching them as they artfully spun their webs. Their penchant for wrapping their victims in silk and sucking them dry was also a source of great fascination.

One day, as I was walking toward the Fayu village, I noticed a bright glimmer out of the corner of my eye. Irresistibly drawn to it, I noticed the largest spider web I had ever seen in a bush at the edge of the jungle. The web covered the entire bush. My heart beat faster, and I forgot why I was going to the village. What sort of spider could have built such a masterpiece? I didn't have to search long; in the middle of the web was a huge spider, rivaling the size of those we encountered in our house on the first day.

It was a lovely creature. The shape was unusual – not the typical oval, but a narrow rectangular shape. It resembled a snake in its brilliantly shimmering colours: black, blue, red and many other colours. The spider hovered motionless in the centre of its web. I carefully approached and pulled a strand off the web, but the strand was so strong that I wasn't able to tear it in two. I could barely believe my luck!

Excited, I ran back to the house to find the largest jar I could in which to catch the spider. But even the largest jar was too small. Aside from that, alarm bells were starting to ring in my head as I remembered that brilliant colours on an animal or plant often meant it was poisonous. So I contented myself with simply watching it for a while.

The next day, my admiration of the spider went up another notch. As soon as I had finished my schoolwork, I ran outside to visit the spider, whom I had named Rainbow. As I neared the bush, I noticed, much to my astonishment, that a small bird was caught in the web. It fluttered madly but couldn't free itself. Feeling great pity for its plight, I went to free it but froze when I noticed the spider. It was hidden behind a few leaves, watching us. Fear arose in me. Would it attack me if I approached the bird? I kept a respectful distance from it.

The bird's flapping grew weaker, when suddenly the spider shot out of hiding and attacked it. Within a few seconds, the bird fell still. At that moment, my mother called me. With a last glance at the spectacle, I reluctantly obeyed. By the time I came back, the spider had completely wrapped up the bird and was sitting on it.

I looked forward with a sort of horrified fascination to watching Rainbow's future conquests. But the next day when I went back to the bush, there was nothing to see. Everything was gone – the spider, the web and even the bird. Whether a Fayu or some animal was responsible for this, I cannot say. But I was terribly disappointed. On the other hand, maybe this was for the best. Who knows what Rainbow would have done to my animal collection.

My disappointment didn't last long. There were many other fascinating attractions that could grab the attention of a jungle child . . .

12

BOW AND ARROW

Christian and I were once again outside playing with our bows and arrows. As we got older, we outgrew the ones that Tuare had given us. So we were fashioning larger bows with the help of our friends. Larger bows require larger arrows, so those were next on the list to construct.

'Hey Sabine, come help me string my bow,' Christian called.

'Not right now – I want to finish my arrows first,' I replied.

He got angry and continued to nag me. In irritation, I finally took his bow and began to string it. We had been arguing all day and were on edge with one another. As I was working on Christian's bow, he began playing with mine. I got angry. 'Babu, put that down. It's mine.'

I turned back to stringing his bow when he suddenly notched an arrow and shot at me. The arrow hit me in the elbow and penetrated to the bone. I screamed like a stuck pig, started to cry, and rolled on the ground in pain. Papa came running. He immediately saw what had happened and pulled the arrow out of my arm.

'It was an accident! It was an accident!' Christian screamed in fear and regret.

'No!' I screamed back. 'You were trying to kill me!' The wound burned like fire.

Papa was beside himself with anger. He grabbed all of our arrows and broke off the tips. In the meantime, several Fayu had assembled around us and were watching with interest to see how Papa would handle it.

Papa carried me into the house. I was bawling as Christian ran behind us, also crying his eyes out. Mama took him to task as she bandaged my arm.

We weren't allowed to have any tips on our arrows for a month. Eventually, though, it was forgotten. Despite my screams blaming him, I never for a moment considered that Christian shot me with bad intentions. It was a child's accident in the jungle. Nothing more. And eventually we got to use arrows with tips again.

The bow and arrow were among the most valuable possessions of the Fayu. They were used for hunting, self-defence and to take revenge. The bow was sized to its user. Men had bows that were up to half a yard taller than themselves. They were fashioned out of hardwood and were strung with bamboo twine.

There were three primary types of arrow tips: wood, bamboo and bone. The wooden tip, named *zehai*, was used for hunting small animals and birds. The *bagai* arrow, made of bamboo, was for hunting wild pigs and ostriches. This was a wide-tipped arrow, designed to cause the animal to bleed more heavily so that death was quicker. The *fai* tip was made from wallaby bones and was designed to kill people.

The hunter's bow was decorated with various bird feathers – trophies of previous kills. Every hunter crafted his own arrows and carved his identifying sign into them to leave no doubt as to whose arrow killed the prey. As children, we often admired the elaborate designs that resulted.

However pretty they may have been, they caused much grief. Several times I even saw children attack adults with bow and arrows when they were angry over not getting their way.

Even Papa was threatened several times. Once, a young man lost his temper, notched an arrow, and aimed to kill him. But then Papa reacted unexpectedly. He slowly walked directly toward the man and hugged him. This was something the Fayu had never seen before. The white man's behaviour was so surprising, so inappropriate in the Fayu worldview, that the man didn't know how to react. Papa wasn't hurt that time or ever.

But we always tried to exercise caution. Papa was careful not to violate the Fayu's social code or lose his temper with a Fayu. We could never be entirely sure of their reaction to situations, so we were very careful not to stumble onto hidden taboos.

13

THE SEASONS
OF THE JUNGLE

One day I ran home, parched from playing all day. I filled a glass with water and began to drink thirstily, but there was a weird taste to the water. I set the glass down and noticed that the water had a brown colouring, but otherwise seemed okay. So I drank some more, but soon the taste got to me. I asked my brother to try it. He took one sip and immediately spat it back out. We went and tried it with Papa, who had the same reaction.

Papa thought that maybe something was wrong with our rain drums. We all went to the platform where they were mounted and climbed up to have a look. Christian suddenly made a face and called out to me as he looked into one of the drums. I climbed over to him to see what he had discovered. Floating on top of the water was a fat, half-rotted frog. We could see its intestines and the little white worms that were industriously at work on its carcass. We quickly emptied the containers and cleaned them. Now we just had to hope for rain to restock our water supply.

There are only two types of weather in the rain forest: the rainy season and the dry season. During the dry season, it was sometimes so hot that we had to stay in the house. By early morning, one could all ready feel the heat that blanketed man and animal alike. Animals would crawl away and hide in their nests and holes in the cool underbrush of the forest. The advantage to this was that there weren't many critters in the house.

I spent most of this time in the water to keep cool. But when it hadn't rained for a while, the water level fell drastically. This created sandbanks in the river, which then became a new playground. The sandbanks sometimes expanded to the point that the river would almost disappear from sight. The narrow stream of water that remained ran deep and flowed quickly, and so we had to be careful not to venture out too far.

The sandbank that we had to cross in order to get home got so hot that it would blister our feet if we tried to walk on it barefoot. We often forgot our flip-flops – a circumstance that left us stranded in the water on the far side of the riverbed. That left a singular strategy: standing there pathetically, calling out to Mama for help. She would usually send Minius to save us, who would either bring us our flip-flops or carry us across the sandbank, grinning with that look of kind indulgence that he reserved for us non-natives.

The nights were the worst part of the dry season for me. They were barely cooler than the day, and the humidity seemed particularly oppressive. At some point, I developed a system that made it possible for me to sleep. I would lie on my back near the edge of the bed. After a couple of minutes, when that spot became too hot, I'd turn on my stomach and lay on a cool patch of sheet until that also became uncomfortable; then I'd roll again. In this way, I travelled from one side of the bed to the other in constant search of a cool spot until I fell asleep.

If it happened to be a full moon, its brightness made sleeping even more difficult. The moon shined so brightly that it seemed to never get really dark. That could make for long, restless nights.

And then, when I thought the heat wave would never end, relief came in the form of the rainy season. Its arrival was usually signalled by a mighty thunderstorm. One morning, I got up – the air all ready oppressive – ate my breakfast, did my schoolwork, and went outside to play. As I was splashing in the river with Tuare, Foni and Abusai, I happened to glance up and noticed huge, black clouds building on the horizon. They are unlike anything you see in the West. The clouds form dark, towering banks that look like a mountain range in the otherwise blue sky. They stand out rather ominously and convey a raw sense of power.

I climbed out of the water in order to get a better view of the coming storm, my eyes never leaving the fantastic scenario. The mountain of clouds grew closer with startling speed. All ready I could hear the first rumblings of thunder and see the lightning that flashed from the midst of the clouds. Closer and closer it came. There was a sudden flash of incredibly bright lightning, accompanied by a terrific boom that shook the ground. Within seconds, everything grew dark, and a strong wind full of static energy swept over me.

I felt a large raindrop on my skin. Splash! Then another one. Then three or four at once. And then the heavens opened up. It rained with the power of the great flood. I spread my arms, closed my eyes, and turned my face upward toward the sky. What a remarkable sensation that was. Lightning, thunder, wind and rain. The raindrops were the size of pebbles and fell with a force that hurt.

Swallowed by the storm, I felt one with nature. The heat was chased away as refreshing coolness spread over the land. I didn't move as the rain whipped my body and the wind wrapped its arms around me. Then I heard Mama's voice calling for me to come in the house.

Judith, who had not forgotten the snake incident, was watching from the doorway. 'Oh, Mama,' she said, 'let her be. Maybe we'll get lucky and she'll be hit by lightning.'

Mama was shocked by this remark and reprimanded my sister. But I understood Judith as only a sister could – her life would have been easier without me, on occasion.

By this time, all of the people had found shelter in their huts. I ran to our house. I had barely stepped inside when lightning flashed so brightly that we were all blinded for a few seconds. I immediately sank to the floor and covered my ears in anticipation of what was about to happen. The explosion of sound was so loud that it felt like it knocked our house down. Before the sound could die away, there was another flash of lightning and roll of thunder. Then another, and another. It stormed so loudly, we could barely hear ourselves think. After a few minutes, the front edge of the storm passed by, leaving only the rain.

I stood up and looked out the window. It was dark as night, and the rain was so thick, I could barely recognize anything, like a curtain that drew itself over the jungle. And so it went on for quite a while. The river regained its fullness, and the thirsty ground was satisfied.

The first day of the rainy season was always a welcome change. We could sleep easily again and could breathe deeply without feeling suffocated. But we were cooped up during the day. We obviously had no television, not many toys and no commercial radio. We only had a Walkman with a couple of cassettes and a few books that we had all ready read more than once.

So we would sit for days on our beds, listening to music or reading the stories we all ready knew by heart. We lay around, listening to the storm, counting the seconds between lightning and thunder, as all children do. If the centre of the storm was directly over us, we would have to plug our ears because of the thunder and the deafening sound of the heavy rain on our aluminium roof. When the rain abated enough, Mama would read us books in German to improve our language skills.

Man, was I bored during these times! The rain would only last a couple of days, but it seemed like an eternity to me. We could only play outside in the rain for short periods of time before the lightning would chase us back into the house.

The Fayu also stayed in their huts. During the rainy season, they seldom went hunting, so there was little meat or fish on the menu. Since we did not hunt ourselves, we depended on the Fayu to obtain meat that they would then trade to us for such useful items as fishhooks, knives, pots or clothing. During this 'lean' season, we made do with canned vegetables, biscuits and rice or sweet potatoes.

Sometimes when it seemed to rain for days on end, we all grew moody. The only one who would enjoy these times was Judith. She had discovered that the tips of burnt wood made excellent pencils for sketching, so she saved up a large supply to use during this time.

First, Judith drew family portraits. When Mama refused to give her more paper, the walls became her canvas. Judith created large landscapes complete with Fayu figures so realistic they seemed to be alive. Joyfully, Judith would draw for hours without concern for anything else.

Many years later, after Judith had started her professional art career, she told me about the first time she visited an art supply store. When she saw their vast array of charcoal pencils, she felt a deep sense of disappointment. 'For all those years, I believed I was the first person to discover that coal could be used for sketching,' she told me with a smile.

Early one morning during a rainy season, my brother shook me awake and told me to look out the window. I looked and saw nothing but water everywhere. I couldn't see the ground any more, as the river had overflowed its banks; this was our first big flood. We were hugely excited and turned to make our way to the door. But we never made it that far.

As I turned around, I froze. The walls and floors appeared to be moving – thousands of spiders, ants, beetles and other assorted insects covered them. Apparently, the insects had all chosen our house as the place to seek shelter from the flood. I swallowed hard. Much as I liked insects, this was too much even for me. I stood without moving and called loudly for Mama. She jumped out of her bed, stepped into the room, and froze in horror.

Imagine for a moment getting up in the morning as usual and going to the kitchen to make coffee. You reach for the coffee can but grab a handful of spiders. You try to turn on the faucet, and an army of ants conquers your arm. You take a look around, and all of the furniture, the recently scrubbed floor, your shower, coffeepot, pot and pans – everything, everything! – is covered in insects. That's what our house was like.

Mama cried desperately for Papa to wake up. In the meantime, Christian and I had recovered from our shock and began to look around with interest. Whenever either one of us discovered a new type of insect, we announced it to each other. And naturally, we soon had a brilliant idea involving Judith, who was sleeping innocently, as she slept deeply and was hard to wake up. We crept up to the edge of her bed.

'Hey Judith, wake up. We have a surprise for you!' I called out with unusual glee.

Judith turned to me and murmured sleepily, 'This better not be one of your mean tricks.' With a skeptical expression, she climbed out of bed. Christian was hiding behind me, trying to suppress his giggling.

'Come along! Mama and Papa are awake too,' I lured her with the most innocent expression I could master. Judith wandered groggily to the bedroom door, where I exclaimed, 'Take a look! We have some visitors.'

Judith suddenly became aware of her surroundings and let out a bloodcurdling scream. Christian and I fell to the floor laughing. Mama wasn't quite as amused. As punishment, I had to bring Judith breakfast in bed, where she spent the rest of the day under the mosquito net.

In the meantime, Mama and Papa had armed themselves with bug spray and flyswatters and went to work clearing the inside of the house. I tried helping, but after a while, my mother threw me out with the remark that I was being counterproductive.

I had no idea what she meant. I was simply trying to save the poor creatures. While Mama and Papa continued in their murderous ways, I collected everything that moved and threw it outside. The obvious flaw in my plan was that they crawled right back into the house, so my mother banned me and Christian (my most loyal assistant) to the landing outside the house. We went to the stairs that lead down to the ground. The water level was almost up to the top step. Water covered everything – the helicopter landing pad, the village, simply everything. Small branches and debris floated past us, coated in ants.

It had stopped raining, and the sun shone down warmly. I clambered down the steps and into the water. The brown wetness came up to my stomach. The ground was slippery, and I had to be careful not to fall. Christian stayed on the stairs because the water was too deep for him. I sloshed around for a long while, helping the ants get onto the trees, feeling like the guardian angel of insects.

But the real fun began the next day! The flooding had disappeared by the time we woke up, the water having receded back into the river. I was so excited, I could barely concentrate on my schoolwork. As soon as we were done, the three of us flew outside. The Fayu kids were all ready waiting for us. The ground was very muddy, which inspired our imagination. We built our first jungle slide, which later on became one of our favourite activities. We looked for a spot on the riverbank that was free of bushes. Having settled on a site, we cleared it of debris and smoothed it with our hands until it formed an even, slippery path. Then we'd get a running start, jump, and slide on our backsides down the path and into the river. Splash! Occasionally we would add a few curves, just to keep it interesting.

At the beginning, the Fayu just watched us, perhaps questioning our sanity. But after a while, some of them tried it out themselves, and soon word got around. Before long, there were lines of people waiting for a turn.

It was great fun. We were covered top to bottom with mud; our blond hair was brown and our skin resembled that of the Fayu. Only our blue eyes distinguished us from the natives.

14

THE CYCLE OF DEATH

Although we enjoyed nature and its myriad diversions, we found even greater joy in watching the Fayu children learn to laugh. With us, they discovered the childhood that had been stolen from them by hate, fear and tribal war. Since their earliest childhood, fear was the Fayu's primary emotion. In time, we came to understand the reasons for this.

The Fayu believed in only two causes of death. A person either died from an arrow wound or as the result of a curse. Because they lacked any medical understanding of sickness or infection, they believed that a human could not die of natural causes, attributing symptoms to spiritual or magical causes.

If a member of my family or clan died of disease, it would be my duty to determine who cursed that person. Then I would be forced to avenge my relative. For example, an Iyarike would have an argument with a Tigre. A short while later, the Iyarike might die a natural death (e.g., from malaria). The immediate assumption would be that the Tigre must have cursed the person who died in retaliation for the argument they had. The Iyarike would then be obligated to kill the first available (ie, most vulnerable) Tigre. The result of this was that all Fayu – men, women and children – were vulnerable to being picked off as part of the blood feud. And grudges were kept for decades, so you never knew when that cycle of violence might find you. Hence, the Fayu lived in perpetual anxiety.

The other explanation for death, an arrow, was therefore usually the result of an act of revenge. If I were a Fayu warrior and a member of a different clan killed my brother, then I, along with my entire family and clan, would have the obligation to avenge his death, the same as if we believed they had cursed him with some disease. The retribution would not be limited to the offending party but could justifiably include any member of his clan. For the purposes of the blood feud, people within a clan were viewed as interchangeable, and *any* death would satisfy the demand for revenge. In turn, that clan would be obligated to avenge the death of the person I killed, and thus continued the cycle of violence.

Marriage added a whole other layer to the cycle. Chiefs were responsible for obtaining wives for the men of their clan. The most common practice was to get a wife from outside one's own clan, as marriageable women tended to be in short supply. (This shortage was due, in part, to the practice of polygamy and the high rate of mortality during childbirth.) Getting a woman from another clan usually involved murdering the man who protected her – whether that was her father, brother or husband. She, along with any of her children, would then be kidnapped and given to the man who needed a wife. And, in keeping with the cycle of violence, the death of the protector would then have to be avenged by his clan members.

And so the cycle became increasingly brutal. By the time we arrived among the Fayu, it had gotten to the point where opposing clan members met only to kill.

As time passed and the Fayu fell further and further into the grip of revenge and murder, their population dwindled from the thousands down to several hundred. And so they developed a culture singularly focused on revenge, without mercy or tender affection.

Children who grew up in this culture of hate knew no security or innocence. Those things were robbed in the moment the children witnessed loved ones being tortured and killed. On the occasions when both parents were killed, their children were sometimes left to wander around the jungle. If they weren't found by members of their own clan, they would eventually die of starvation or fall prey to the various dangers the jungle posed.

One day while we were living in Foida, Papa ran into the house with great urgency. 'I have to go upriver immediately. There are three little boys left alone in the jungle.' Chief Baou had murdered a man and his wife from the Iyarike clan as part of the continuing blood feud. He killed and dismembered the couple in front of their children and then left the traumatized boys there with the bodies.

With tears in my eyes I pleaded, 'Mama, can't we adopt the three boys since they don't have parents any more?'

Mother explained to me that in the Fayu culture, the children would have to be adopted by a family of the same clan. To distract me and make me feel like I could be helpful, she suggested that I pick out presents for the boys. I found fishing hooks and line and a small pocketknife for each of the boys. But was that enough? I felt so much pain in my heart; I wanted to give them something special. So I chose to give them my greatest treasure – my collection of coloured marbles.

Papa left with some Fayu men to go look for the kids. After several hours, they returned with three small boys aged between three and seven. Fear and horror were etched on their faces. In an effort to comfort Diro and his brothers, I gave them my gifts but recognized that they were in no state to appreciate them. They were completely paralyzed by the brutality they had just witnessed, and they jumped at every noise.

The Iyarike men called for an assembly of their clan. After a long discussion that lasted into the night, three families each adopted one of the boys. The pain of this separation stayed with me for a long time. I took the boys a bowl of rice every day in an attempt to alleviate their pain and help me cope with my own grief.

In a world of such horrors, it is no wonder that Fayu children tended to stay near their parents or sit with their backs against a tree. Living in a state of constant low-grade fear leaves little room for games and laughter. Fayu children didn't run around playing. They knew little love, no forgiveness and no peace, and they had no hope for a better future.

What Teau had told my father on their first meeting was true. The Fayu actually did long for peace and an end to the killing and war, even though they continued to participate in the cycle of violence. But because they were bound by the ancient law of revenge, they didn't know what else to do. They couldn't find a way out of the cycle.

Our arrival provided a loophole for them. More important than the fact that our skin was a different colour or that we came from a different 'tribe' was the fact that we stood outside of their blood feud. Our house was neutral territory. Trading trips to visit us provided a way for clans to be present in the same territory without being obligated to go to war. Over time, they learned to talk with one another again. They started sharing food and hunting stories. It would take many years before the cycle of violence was completely broken, but the first step had been taken.

Judith, Christian and I played a role in that initial step. With us, the Fayu children got a taste of a different world, where they could forget about the constant threat of violence. In play, they became like us – happy children.

One testimony to the progress of peace is that years later, when Mama opened up the first Fayu school, children from the different clans attended classes together. Two of her students were Diro (one of the boys orphaned by Chief Baou) and Isori, the son of Chief Baou. They were both the same age and highly intelligent.

In the beginning, the two children hated each other. Mama sat them down frequently to discuss their history. With her intervention, their enmity began to decrease. Eventually, the two boys became inseparable friends. Years later, when Isori became chief, he made Diro his closest advisor. Their friendship remains strong to this day.

15

NEWS FROM THE
OUTSIDE WORLD

We sank deeper and deeper into the jungle's rhythms but we were never completely immersed in them. Besides our regular visits to Danau Bira, we also got mail delivered to Foida every couple of months, which would remind us of an outside world. The delivery was always an exciting event – not just for us, but also for the Fayu. My father and the pilot would agree upon the date and exact delivery time several days beforehand. As the event grew closer, our anticipation escalated.

'I'm going to get lots of letters this time,' Judith said joyfully. She always perked up when the mail was coming.

'Me, too! Me, too!' I echoed with enthusiasm.

'Oh, Sabine!' Judith sighed, rolling her eyes. 'You aren't going to get any letters because you never write any. Didn't Mama explain that to you last time?'

What Mama had explained to me went unprocessed by my eight-year-old brain. I simply couldn't cope with delayed gratification. It would take a minimum of two months to receive a reply to a letter, and so I didn't write any.

'Surely I'll get a letter this time anyway,' I said with a mix of defiance and childlike trust in the justice of the world.

The mail generally didn't arrive until the afternoon, but by midmorning, Mama always had to give up on school-work. Our excitement overwhelmed our concentration.

'Is it here yet? When is he getting here?' asked Christian. He had been waiting for hours in front of the house. Papa didn't even bother to answer this time. We had all ready asked him a hundred times over. He just whistled to himself as he always did when he was trying to ignore someone. This method didn't work very well with Christian. He had more endurance than any of us.

The Fayu grew excited. They could all ready hear the motor of the small aeroplane. A few minutes later, the rest of us could hear the faint drone coming closer. I eagerly scanned the sky, shading my eyes from the sun. There! The small dot in the sky was the Cessna we were waiting for.

The whole village waved as it flew over us. The plane banked and turned back toward the village as it descended. Papa watched the tips of the trees to gauge the wind cur-rents. We all held our breath. The plane was piloted by an American named Rex, who lived with his family in Danau Bira. Skimming the tops of the trees, he opened his window as he got near us. I could easily recognize 'Uncle' Rex as he extended his arm out the window and dropped the mail-bag.

Now the real fun began as we raced to see who could reach the bag first. The bag narrowly missed the water. We all cheered as it landed on a sandbank. The previous deliv-ery had landed in the river, and even the plastic wrapping on the letters hadn't prevented water damage. It had taken a long time to dry everything, and much of it ended up being unreadable.

The winner of the race brought us our mail, doing a joyful jig. This image often comes to mind now when I see my mailman making his way through the neighbourhood. I wonder what he would think of our jungle system.

We always used the delivery of the mail as an excuse for a celebration, with dance, food and storytelling. In the Fayu culture, there were no celebrations or feasts – not for birthdays or any other occasion. So we used any excuse to have a party.

Mama usually had a very large pot of rice ready. Together with the Fayu, we would sit and eat around one of the fires that burned here and there throughout the village. Then Mama and Papa would go back into the house and open their letters. Today, I can understand how important those letters were for my parents. It was their only contact with their homeland. They must have longed often for news from friends and relatives back home.

On this delivery day, I was the only one who did not receive a letter. Not even one from my beloved grandmother in Germany. With great sorrow, I lay down on my bed.

Judith took pity on me. 'Sabine,' she said. 'Look, I got five letters this time. I don't need all of them, so why don't you take one.' Then she gave me a pretty purple envelope covered with stamps. Thankful – and completely uninterested in the contents – I gave her a slobbery kiss on the cheek and ran out the door. I wanted to show my treasure to Bebe and Tuare. Man, would they be impressed!

16

JUNGLE DANGERS

One morning, as we were dashing between the trees in front of the house, I heard a piercing scream. I froze instantly, trying to discern the direction of the sound, but my hearing wasn't as well trained as that of Bebe and Tuare. Bebe grabbed my arm with surprising strength and pulled me to the nearest tree. I didn't know what was happening but had learned to trust their instincts. We climbed the tree at top speed. Securely in the tree, I noticed Christian sitting calmly by a fire. I yelled out to him to climb a tree as quickly as possible. We had been trained to obey such directives without question, so he immediately did as I said. He was barely off the ground when a herd of wild boars raced past us toward the helicopter landing pad.

From my vantage point, I could see a single Fayu man slowly meandering toward the village. I couldn't understand why he wasn't running or climbing a tree. Surely he must have heard the squealing pigs and the warning cry. Maybe these pigs belonged to him, and that's why he wasn't scared.

The Fayu had a very specific way of dealing with pigs. To tame a piglet, a Fayu would hold it next to his skin for three days, never letting it go. He would talk to the piglet, rub its tummy (a pig's favourite spot), feed it and sleep with it. After this period, the piglet recognized this person as his master. The pig was then let go and would wander freely in the wild. Months could pass without contact, but the animals would still recognize their masters. Any person other than the owner would be in danger of being attacked, as only the 'master' was recognized by the pig. The Fayu would do this to several pigs, and thus a herd was created that was semi-wild.

As I watched the herd of pigs closing in on the man, I felt that something was terribly wrong. He should be responding in some way, even if these were his pigs. The pigs were only a few yards from him when he happened to glance around. My heart stopped when I recognized him. It was Nakire's brother, who was deaf and mute.

The herd overran him, and he crashed to the ground before he could make a sound. I closed my eyes but could still hear the squeals of the enraged animals as they attacked with their tusks. A couple of Fayu men came running past my tree with bow and arrow in hand. But what could they do? Killing another Fayu's pigs was forbidden – even to save a human being. Thankfully, the owner of the pigs came running out of the village, jumped into the middle of the herd and shooed them away.

Mama had heard the commotion and came running to help. Once the wild boars disappeared back into the forest, we climbed down from the tree and ran over to Nakire's brother. He was lying in the grass, bleeding profusely from several wounds, but was still alive. Mama took out her medical supplies and started treating him. He made the only sounds he could – unintelligible moans. I felt so sorry for him even though I didn't really like him. Thanks to Mama's ministrations, he didn't develop any infections and soon recovered.

This incident reminded us to be cautious and to always be aware of the location of the nearest tree in case we needed to climb it. Despite that, we had several more close calls over the years. One incident I remember vividly involved my sister, Judith. It hadn't rained for days, and so a large sandbank developed in front of our house. We were using it for a game in which we pretended we were mining for gold.

I took a handful of promising rocks into the house to store in my backpack. When I came back outside, a small herd of pigs was standing between our house and the river. I called out a warning to Judith, who was still playing on the sandbank. The onlooking Fayu had all ready climbed trees. Suddenly one of the wild boars looked over at the sandbank, and the entire herd swung in that direction.

Throughout the years, the Fayu had rescued us from dangers on numerous occasions, and they tried again this time. They started swinging their arms and shouting loudly to scare off the pigs. But they were too far away. I watched wide-eyed as a scenario unfolded that, in hindsight, is quite funny. There was my big sister, with her long ponytails flapping out behind her as she raced along the sandbank. The herd of pigs chased her, and a group of Fayu warriors chased them. And then came Papa, bringing up the rear as fast as he could. Once again coming to the rescue, he yelled out, 'Into the water! Jump into the water!'

Judith hooked left and threw herself into the river. The herd of wild boars rushed past her. It was as though they had just wanted to scare her.

Incidents like this weren't uncommon, and over the years, we learned to react better and more quickly. Eventually, we didn't need a pack of warriors to come to our rescue; we managed to avoid trouble ourselves. My instincts developed to the point that I could sense danger before there was any obvious warning sign. I learned to read nature, to judge situations by listening to the sounds of the jungle and the animals in it, to recognize the smallest changes in the atmosphere. The local animals have phenomenal instincts and amazing senses and can even predict earthquakes and storms. Learning to interpret their behaviour and vocalizations could give one advance warning of danger.

We had another close call once as we were playing tag on the shore. The Fayu children played along with enthusiasm, although they didn't really grasp the game. We tried to explain the game in a way that fit their culture and so called it 'boar hunting'. One person was the hunter, while the rest of us were the boars. If the hunter managed to tag one of the boars, he in turn would become the hunter. This confused the Fayu kids. Shouldn't the boar then be dead? After careful deliberation, we decided that our version of the game was better. The Fayu kids were faster than us, and we didn't feel like lying around all day playing dead boar.

So we raced about the landscape, going around and under our house, past the little hut where Papa was desperately trying to concentrate on the complicated tone variations of the Fayu language. Christian was currently the hunter and was chasing me, since I was the slowest of the boars. I devised a plan of escaping over the water and ran like the wind toward the riverbank.

As I hurdled over the brush to land on the sandbank, I heard a shout of warning. Still flying through the air, I noticed a large snake directly under me, warming itself in the sun. I realized that landing on the snake could very well be the end of me. But how could I avoid it?

I still don't know how I managed it. Suddenly, it was as if time slowed down; everything seemed to move in slow motion. Within a split second, I came up with a plan. I twisted in the air and spread out my arms and legs, landing on all fours with the snake directly under my stomach. Snakes will attack any movement when threatened. But since I had landed in four places at once, it paused momentarily in confusion. This gave me just enough time to kick out and roll away from danger.

Afterward I felt untouchable. Full of pride, I ran to Mama and told her how a huge, poisonous snake had almost killed me. She smiled politely, thinking this was another flight of imagination.

The incident did teach me to be more careful, and I appreciated more fully the basic safety rules of the jungle: never reach where you cannot see. For example, you shouldn't reach under a log or behind a tree without looking first, since you do not know whether a scorpion, centipede or snake may be lurking there. And never take a blind step without verifying first that you're not about to step on something sharp or poisonous.

I didn't wear closed shoes very often, so it took me a while to learn to always shake out my shoes before putting them on. Whenever I forgot, the squashed cockroaches and spiders served as useful reminders. A number of times, scorpions, spiders or other insects fell out of my clothing as I shook them out. It didn't take very long for these basic precautions to become automatic.

I don't want to give the impression that there was a poisonous creature under every leaf, merely that one never knew if this was the case. And we learned that animals or poisonous insects generally only attack when threatened. As long as we didn't surprise them, kept our distance and respected their territory, there was no real danger. We also learned that pleasant things, such as the river or a campfire, could pose significant dangers. Twice we almost lost Christian this way.

The first time Christian was about six years old. The Fayu had slaughtered a wild boar and built a bonfire in preparation for smoking the meat. Christian and I were once again playing tag with the Fayu children. We darted back and forth in a frantic attempt to outrun the speedy Fayu.

'Babu, Sabine! Watch out for the fire,' Papa called out as we raced past him. He was sitting in a circle of warriors, working on his linguistic studies.

Christian and I didn't really pay attention, as we were too engrossed in our game. I was the hunter and had almost caught up with him when he dashed around one side of the fire, slipped, and fell headlong into it. Burning pieces of wood flew in all directions as the flames engulfed his little body.

Papa jumped up with a yell and literally flew across the ground toward us. Within a fraction of a second, he snatched his burning son from the fire and jumped into the river. Despite his speed, Papa's clothes were smoking. I froze and began screaming. Mama rushed out of the house and saw the Fayu running around, not knowing how to help.

'Christian fell into the fire!' I cried.

Mama jumped down the stairs and ran to the river. My very pale father was slowly coming out of the water, carrying my screaming brother in his arms. He gave Christian to Mama, who carried him into the house. When she undressed him, she saw that he had thankfully only suffered very small, minor burns in various places.

But the shock of it stayed with us for a long time. If Papa hadn't been so near or hadn't reacted so quickly, we could easily have lost Christian. Even if we could have gotten him to the capital city of Jayapura, the hospital there did not have the ability to deal with major burns. From that moment on, our cooking fire was built in a clearing behind our house, where we were not allowed to play.

We also learned that water could be as dangerous as fire. We had always loved the Klihi River, which was just a few yards from our house. We would frequently jump into the water to cool ourselves off. Since the water came from the small mountains in the distance, it was cold by tropical standards. When we were sufficiently refreshed, we would let the sun warm us up again.

My parents recognized the potential danger of the river and frequently warned us not to stray out of the shallow, slow-moving water at the edge – a caution we actually paid attention to in the beginning. The current of the river was so strong that a grown man was not able to swim against it and could be dragged off his feet without a chance of regaining his balance. Over time, however, we became braver (or less prudent, as my mother would say).

The danger wasn't always the speed of the current but the nature of the riverbanks. In some parts, the banks are so high and slippery that one can't climb them without slipping back into the water. At other spots, the vegetation grew very thick and extended out into the water so that one couldn't get past it to find solid ground. You could hang onto a branch or a clump of weeds, but eventually your strength would fade and you would end up back in the current. So even strong swimmers faced a real possibility of drowning.

One particular morning, Christian and I were playing in the river with a few other children. It had rained the previous day, and the river flowed high and fast. We were playing some chasing game, and I swam out into the fast current, farther than I was supposed to, in an effort to escape Christian. I was bigger and stronger than him and had no trouble swimming against the current.

As he chased right behind me, his strength suddenly gave out, and the current took him. I tried to hang onto his arm, but I wasn't strong enough, and his arm slipped out of my grip. I could only watch with dismay as the fast current bore him downstream and he cried out for help. The other kids tried to reach him, but he was moving too fast. Panicked, I started screaming, 'Babu, Babu, Babu!' over and over.

We were not allowed to scream except in an emergency, so when Papa heard me, he came racing out of his little office hut. He immediately recognized the danger his son was in and sprinted to the motorboat. Papa yanked on the starter cable like a man possessed, but as always seemed to happen when it was needed most, the motor didn't want to start.

The Fayu men ran along the shoreline, calling out and trying to keep Christian in sight. But soon they reached a spot where the dense vegetation prohibited passage. Mama and Judith had also come running out of the house and stood helplessly by the riverside.

Christian continued to be swept downstream toward the curve, just barely managing to keep his head above water. Once he reached the curve, we would lose sight of him from the bank. It would even be difficult for Papa to find him again from his vantage point in the boat since the water was so muddy.

Finally the motor caught, and Papa raced out into the centre of the river, where the current was quickest. He sped downriver as Christian drew closer and closer to the curve.

The river narrowed there, and the current became even quicker. Suddenly, his head disappeared under the water. I couldn't stop screaming. Judith stood there crying, while Mama desperately ran down the river's edge, calling out for her son.

Papa reached the spot where Christian had gone under and frantically looked around. He caught sight of Christian's head as it surfaced a little ways downstream and immediately turned the boat toward him. Just as he grabbed Christian by the arm, they disappeared around the curve in the river. Everyone fell silent, barely daring to breathe.

I stared at the spot where they had disappeared until my eyes started burning from not blinking, in fear that I would miss something. After what seemed like a terribly long while, the boat rounded the curve carrying Papa, who had Christian sitting on his lap. I couldn't stop the tears of relief from flooding down my face.

Mama jumped into the water before the boat even reached the shore. She lifted Christian out and wrapped him in a blanket that Minius brought. His lips were blue, and his entire body was shaking. He was in shock and completely limp. Mama carried Christian into the house, undressed him and laid him on the bed. After a hot cup of tea, colour slowly returned to his face.

Papa was still very pale as he went around reassuring the many Fayu who had gathered around. He told them everything was fine, but it was quite a while before he was able to fully believe it himself.

The rest of the day passed very quietly. We were so grateful that Christian was still alive. The experience taught us a convincing lesson. It wasn't until we were several years older that we ventured back into the danger of the deepest currents.

17

DORIS AND
DORISO BOSA

I must have been about ten when my mother took on a new task with the Fayu. We were sitting at the table for a meal when we heard screaming and moaning from the other side of the river. From the window, we could see Biya standing in the water. Papa went outside to ask what was going on.

'She's about to give birth,' Nakire answered, as though it was self-evident.

'By herself? In the river?' Papa asked with surprise.

Nakire covered his mouth with his hand and said, 'I am mute.' This was the Fayu way of indicating that they could not talk about a subject. It is a Fayu taboo for men to talk about birth or be near it.

So Papa went to Chief Kologwoi and asked for permission to violate the taboo long enough to transport Mama across the river so she could help Biya. Chief Kologwoi agreed. When the boat arrived on the other side of the river, Biya was still standing in the water – presumably so that the coolness of the water would dull her labour pains. The first thing Mama did was pull her out of the river. It was just in the nick of time, as the baby made her appearance shortly thereafter. Delivering this baby girl was the beginning of Mama's career as a Fayu midwife.

That evening, Mama told us what she had learned. A Fayu husband was responsible for building a hut away from the village for his pregnant wife. He would stock it with enough food for a week and then leave until after the birth. Sometimes, an older woman came to attend the delivery.

After Biya's delivery, Mama checked on her and the baby every day. The little girl survived the first several months, which was not a given at the time. The infant mortality rate was around seventy percent. We calculated that a Fayu woman would have approximately six live births in her lifetime. Four of the babies would be lost in the first six months. Another would die before his or her tenth year. This meant that any given Fayu baby had only about a thirty percent chance of living into adulthood.

Because of this mortality rate, the Fayu waited to name a child until its teeth came in. Prior to that point, the baby wasn't considered to be alive. So if you expressed sympathy to a couple who had just lost their newborn, they would act as if they didn't know what you meant – claiming that they had not lost a child. It was the Fayu way of guarding their hearts.

When Biya's daughter got her first tooth, we were proudly told that she had been named Doriso Bosa ('Little Doris'). This was a great honour for Mama. In time, we all had babies named after us.

As a happy endnote, a few years ago, Doriso Bosa and Tuare got married. They now have four healthy children.

18

NAKIRE

During a war between the Dou and Fayu tribes, Nakire and his mother were kidnapped. He was between six and eight at the time. His mother was given as a second wife to a Dou warrior. Although Nakire grew up among the Dou, he was always treated as an outsider. I don't think he had an easy time of it.

When he grew old enough to marry, he started looking around for a wife. But the Dou chieftain told him, 'Get a woman from among your own people. You're an Iyarike and don't belong to us. Go away.' So Nakire took his few possessions, said good-bye to his mother, and disappeared into the jungle.

Shortly after Papa's second expedition, the chief of the Tearue clan called Nakire to himself. He made an offer: 'If you help me to kill an Iyarike in order to avenge my son, I will give you my daughter as a wife.'

To the surprise of all present, Nakire declined the offer. The Tearue chieftain was completely confused. No one had ever rejected such an offer, since marrying a chief's daughter brought status to a man.

Nakire told the chief that he didn't want to kill any more, but wanted to pursue the peace that the white man spoke about. Since he had grown up with the less warlike Dou, Nakire had all ready experienced living in peace and liked it. In the years that he spent with the Dou, Nakire developed the desire to bring peace to his own people.

Nakire became Papa's closest confidante and advised him in matters of culture and language. He taught Papa the basics of the Fayu language, and he would counsel Papa whenever he didn't know how to react to situations.

Toward the beginning of our time with the Fayu, Papa and Nakire were sitting in his office hut, working on linguistics. Papa would point at an object, and Nakire would tell him what it was called in the Fayu language. Then Papa would write it down phonetically. Nakire had never seen paper or pencil before.

Papa had just finished writing his newest word when he noticed that Nakire had grown quiet. Much to Papa's surprise, Nakire was lying on the bench asleep, feet propped up on the table.

'Nakire, what are you doing? You're supposed to help me and instead you are sleeping.'

Nakire sat up, yawning, and said, 'Klausu, I want to help you, but when are you finally going to work? You're just playing around in here.'

'What! I'm playing?' Papa laughed. 'If you don't think of this as work, what do you suggest I do?'

'Well,' Nakire answered, 'a man's job is to go hunting to provide food for his family, or maybe build a new canoe.'

Amused by the image of himself running through the jungle trying to hit something with an arrow, Papa considered how to explain his type of work to Nakire. Then he had an idea. He wrote a note to Mama and told Nakire, 'Please go to Doriso and give her this. She will then bring me something to drink.'

Nakire asked with surprise, 'How is this possible? How will she know to bring you a drink if I don't tell her?'

'The secret is in this piece of paper,' Papa answered.

With skeptical anticipation, Nakire went to the house and gave Mama the note. She read it and did exactly what Papa had prophesied she would do.

Nakire was fascinated. He said, 'I guess it must be important what you are doing in here.'

'That's right!' Papa said. 'Now stop sleeping and help me learn your language.'

Soon after we had moved close to the Fayu, Nakire built a hut across the river from us. A short while after, he found a wife. Her name was Dawai.

One night not long after they got married, we heard pathetic cries from the other side of the river. We were all ready in bed, but the wails kept getting louder, so Papa got up. He lit a kerosene lamp and went outside while the rest of us waited for a report.

After a while, the wailing stopped, and we heard Papa talking to somebody. Then we heard the door open, and Papa came in with Dawai in tow. Her face was swollen and she was crying. 'Nakire hit me!' she told us between sobs. I looked at her with pity. I never would have imagined that Nakire could be capable of such a thing.

Mama gave her something to eat and drink and a place to sleep. I heard Mama and Papa talking long into the night.

The next morning, Papa went outside. Before long, he called out, 'Doris, come quickly!' Mama left the coffee she was preparing and hurried outside. Full of curiosity, I climbed out of bed and went to see what was happening.

Papa and Mama brought Nakire into the house. I recoiled at his appearance. Dried blood and dirt covered his arms and upper body. He looked terrible and was moaning. 'Dawai hit me and then bit me.'

Dawai, who was eating at the table, didn't look up. Without saying a word, Mama began to cleanse and bandage Nakire's wounds. When she was done, Nakire took Dawai's hand, and they silently left the house. Through the window, I saw them return by canoe to their hut.

I never did find out exactly what happened between the two of them. We had assumed that Nakire was the guilty party. It was quite a surprise to find out that Dawai was the instigator. As a child, I was always a little afraid of her. She had a very loud, piercing voice and a temper that even the warriors feared.

When Dawai fell ill a few years later, Papa tried to persuade her to fly with him to the hospital in Jayapura, but she was too afraid of the helicopter and the outside world. My parents and Nakire begged her, but she remained resolute and so we couldn't prevent her death.

Nakire was devastated. He wailed for weeks and in a fit of grief, burned his hut and any possessions that reminded him of her. After that, he spent a lot of time with us. Papa looked after him and tried to comfort him as much as he could.

Over time, Nakire's heart recovered, and he began accompanying Papa on his trips to the Tigre clan. The second Tigre chieftain under Chief Baou had a lovely daughter named Fusai. She was a pretty girl, and her unusual height was considered quite attractive. Nakire fell head over heels in love with her. Every time Papa planned a trip upriver, Nakire would get very excited. He wanted to shower Fusai with gifts and so asked us for things to give her – fishhooks, cloth, jewellery, etc. We happily gave him these items, as it was also the first time we had seen a Fayu man make an effort to win a girl's heart. Usually, a girl was just taken by force, but apparently Nakire was a romantic and wanted to win her affection.

In the course of his efforts, Nakire won not only Fusai's heart but that of her father as well. After several months, the Tigre chief gave his daughter to Nakire in marriage. She was approximately twelve years old, the marrying age for Fayu girls.

Full of pride, Nakire returned with his bride to the Iyarike. With great care he built her a hut near us. It even had walls and a door – a palace by Fayu standards! The first few weeks seemed to go well until early one morning, a panicked Nakire called us all out of bed. Fusai was gone, and he couldn't find her. Immediately, search parties were formed.

The Fayu had developed an excellent long-distance communication system in the jungle. It didn't require cable, machinery or money but simply a loud voice. It was an effective way of transmitting messages over miles. The only disadvantage was that nothing stayed secret. If one sent a message by 'jungle telephone,' everyone in the jungle knew about it.

That system was now put into action on Fusai's behalf. Nakire stood on the riverbank and called upriver in a particular pitch that was more of a howl than a shout. Later, someone explained to me that this pitch carried farther than a simple shout or scream.

'Where is Fusai? Nakire is looking for Fusai,' Nakire repeated several times. After a short while, a second voice could be heard upriver echoing the cry, 'Where is Fusai?

Nakire is looking for Fusai.' The cry was repeated until someone even farther upriver heard it and in turn relayed the message. This continued until it reached the Tigre chief.

'Fusai is with her family,' the answer came, echoing back down the river. Immediately, Papa and Nakire left for the Tigre territory. Nakire was upset and asked Fusai why she had run away. She told him that she had been homesick.

Nakire brought her back to Foida, but a few weeks later, she ran away again. Once again, Nakire had to fetch her back. The third time, he came in frustration to Papa and asked him for advice. What made this surprising was that the Fayu culture provided a ready solution for this type of situation. Normally, a Fayu man would have shot his wife with an arrow with the purpose of wounding her until she obeyed. But Nakire loved Fusai and didn't want to hurt her.

Papa listened to him as Nakire came up with his own solution. The next day, he told us that he would move with Fusai back to her clan until she had gotten used to living with him and was willing to come back to Foida of her own free will.

After several months of living with Fusai and her family in the Tigre territory, Nakire and Fusai returned to Foida. She never ran away again. Fusai was a shy girl with a heart of gold. Her smile was beautiful and we all grew to love her. She was about Judith's age, and the two became best friends. Nakire never took a second wife, as was the custom for Fayu men of high status. He was doubly entitled to do so, since Fusai never bore him a child. But Nakire wanted only her and no one else. Their relationship was unique among the Fayu – the first open love affair. The two have a wonderful marriage that remains alive and well today.

The vast majority of the Fayu men did not treat their wives nearly as well. Twice I witnessed a Fayu wound his wife with an arrow. One of those occasions led me to feel hatred for the first time in my life.

It happened while I was playing outside. Several women were heading into the jungle. The husband of one of the women called her back, but she did not immediately respond. When she finally did step out of the trees, he took his bow, notched an arrow, and shot her in the breast.

The Fayu are excellent marksmen. The husband knew exactly how much pressure to exert on the bowstring so that the arrow would wound but not kill his wife. The woman collapsed, groaning, onto the ground. I felt sick. I wanted to scream, to run away, to kill that man. Everyone could see that this woman was pregnant.

Mama heard the cries and came running out of the house. When she saw the scene, she lost it. I have never seen Mama roar as she did on that day. Mama ran over to the woman, extracted the arrow, and helped her to the house. The man was standing there, laughing at our reactions. I threw him a look of contempt as I followed Mama and the woman into our house. Papa was also very upset, but when he confronted the Fayu about it, they just laughed at him as well.

Today it is different. Over the years, the Fayu watched the relationship between my parents, and what they saw – their respect and love for each other – began to change the way they treated their own wives. It was a new concept for the Fayu that a man and woman could work together, be happy at it and be able to incorporate humour into their relationship. With my parents, they could see how important love was and that arguments didn't have to be settled by arrows or death.

It wasn't until much later that I fully realized the extent to which the Fayu watched us. They understood that we were only human, like them, and that we made mistakes. They witnessed our arguments with one another but also saw that these were settled with apologies and that afterward, the relationships could be restored enough so that we could laugh and play together.

We never told the Fayu how to behave or forced them to adopt our standards of right and wrong. My parents believed, and taught us kids, that the best lesson is the example of one's own life and behaviour. Words alone are empty. You have to live out what you hold to be true. The Fayu needed to decide for themselves whether they wanted to change, for true change comes only from the heart.

19

BOAT EXCURSIONS

Surely this has happened to you: the washing machine breaks, the toaster gives up the ghost, a fuse blows. Naturally, you get upset, but then you get in the car, drive to the nearest store and buy a replacement. With luck, it's still covered by the warranty, so the replacement is free.

But in the jungle, things were a bit more complicated. When something broke, we would have to wait months for a replacement. For example, when the helicopter broke down, replacement parts had to be ordered from the United States, which could take a small eternity. The Indonesian postal system was not very reliable. One time we received a package five years after it had been sent from Germany.

We bought replacement items during resupply trips to Danau Bira. Normally, the helicopter would ferry us directly between Foida and Danau Bira. When the helicopter was out of commission, our only option was to take a canoe to Kordesi, where we would then catch a single-propeller aircraft to Danau Bira. Due to the current, the canoe trip downriver to Kordesi was much faster than the return trip back upriver, which took four to six hours.

We would sit in the long canoe, our supplies distributed between us. Movement required special care, as the canoe tipped over easily. The sun beat down on us, but the light breeze provided some relief. We had to wear long-sleeved shirts and pants to avoid serious sunburn. Every several hours we would stop at a sandbank or an accessible part of the riverbank in order to stretch our legs and eat.

During the long time it took to reach our destination, I would admire the green of the rain forest that lined the banks and the birds that flew overhead. I particularly admired the beautiful orchids of startling red that were known as 'the flame of the jungle'. They grew on vines that wrapped themselves around the trees, and their majestic blooms interrupted the otherwise unending green.

These trips were normally rather boring, and the first several passed without incident. But on the fourth or fifth trip, our luck ran out. As we left Kordesi to begin the return trip upriver, the sun shone brightly and the sky was clear. Mama sat in the front, followed by Judith, Christian and myself, with Papa in the back operating the twelve-horse-power motor. A smaller backup motor lay at his feet in case the larger one failed.

I had made myself comfortable on a pillow. Sitting on wooden planks for hours at a time is taxing on the backside. I wearily swatted at the several flies that were circling my head. After a while, the constant drone of the engine and the heat of the sun lulled me into sleepiness, so I pulled up a sack of rice to use as a pillow for my head.

I don't know how long I slept, but when I woke up, the atmosphere had changed. A sharp, cool breeze blew over us. I looked up at a clear blue sky, but when I looked behind us,

I saw that there were large, threatening clouds amassing in the distance. Papa kept looking worriedly over his shoulder and opened the throttle as wide as it would go. The rest of the family had also noticed the storm, and we all sat completely still in the vain hope that this might increase the canoe's speed.

We merged with the Klihi River, which meant that we were about halfway home. Over the sound of the engine, Papa called out that we might get lucky if the wind shifted. But we all knew that this wasn't very likely. We had a strong tailwind, which meant that the storm front was in hot pursuit.

I tensely watched this display of nature as the sun was swallowed by the clouds. Darkness covered the jungle, and the drone of the engine was the only sound, as nature had grown quiet. Suddenly I felt a drop, then another and soon so many I could not count them any more. Papa's serious expression did not offer me much encouragement about the situation.

We made it around the next curve before the full force of the storm hit us. Papa searched in vain for a place to beach the canoe. There was only dense vegetation that prevented any exit from the river. The raindrops hammered down on me like thousands of small needles. I was soaked through to the skin and was shivering from the cold. I covered my head with my hands as lightning and thunder crashed overhead. I thought it was the end of the world, at least for us.

Mama shouted something, but she was drowned out by the rain and the thunder. I saw her throw a blanket to Christian, who crawled underneath it. Suddenly, I felt something at my feet. At first, I thought it was an animal crawling over my toes, but when I looked down, I saw water. We were sinking!

In that moment, I forgot everything around me, the lightning, the thunder, the raindrops that bore like arrows into my skin. I ripped open a bag containing pots and pans and suddenly realized that that's what Mama had been yelling about before. I distributed the pots to Judith and Mama, and we began bailing as fast as we could.

A race against time began. The downpour was so heavy that the water we bailed out was immediately replaced by fresh rain. I bailed faster and faster. My arms felt like they were about to fall out of their sockets. Through the downpour, I could barely see Judith and Mama's indistinct figures frantically bailing water. Christian was still hidden under the blanket. Papa slowed the boat as visibility became limited to a few yards in front of us. Brilliant lightning punctured the darkness in sporadic bursts.

What a rush! I found myself in the most dangerous moment of my life. The water level in the canoe kept rising despite our best efforts, and the edges of the canoe sank closer and closer to the surface of the river. The current rushing past us seemed eager to swallow us. We were stuck in the grips of a river without mercy.

We kept fighting. The survival instinct drove my body past its limits. Time ceased to exist, and life was reduced to two opposing forces: the power of nature and the strength of our family's will to live.

An odd feeling arose in me – a strange love for the power of the storm, a love for this battle. I felt alive as never before. Every muscle, every cell was fully energized, united in the fight to conquer nature.

As the river threw us into another curve, Papa anxiously searched the riverbanks for landmarks. He had lost all orientation and no longer knew our position along the river. How far had we come? Suddenly, there was a thin, wailing sound that pierced through the noise of the storm raging overhead. At first I thought it was the trees bending in the wind, but the sound continued to grow louder. Papa heard it and carefully steered the canoe closer to the bank of the river. Two figures suddenly appeared, fighting their way through the underbrush at the river's edge. It was the Fayu!

As usual, after dropping us off in Kordesi, the pilot did a quick flyby over the Fayu territory so that they would know we would be arriving within the day. Having heard the sound of the airplane, the Fayu gathered in Foida, awaiting our arrival. They were keenly aware of the dangers of travelling by river in a storm. So, despite the heavy downpour, they waited on the riverbanks to intercept us. Without their help, we would have travelled right past Foida. What a relief it was to see their faces!

As we approached, they jumped into the water and helped secure the canoe. More and more figures appeared out of the storm. One of the men picked me up and carried me to the house. My legs were quivering, and I couldn't move my arms; all the strength had drained out of me. The man set me down on the landing of our house, where I simply collapsed, and then ran back to the boat to help the rest of my family.

In a short while, the boat was unpacked, and we all found ourselves in the protection of our house, cold but greatly relieved. Everything was thoroughly soaked – clothing, schoolbooks, supplies, everything. The only thing that came through the ordeal unharmed was Papa's camera, which he had wrapped in plastic.

We undressed, and Mama brought us dry blankets. She made hot tea and found a tin of biscuits to go with it. I watched the storm through the window and felt as though I had conquered the world. Together we had survived nature's worst. It rained and thundered throughout the night. I snuggled underneath my blanket in the cave of mosquito netting that covered my bed and fell asleep with a smile on my lips.

Later, Papa got an aluminium boat that was delivered to Foida by helicopter. The boat was attached to the helicopter by a long cable, which made for a tense journey. If it had started swinging too much, the pilot would have had to release the cable, dumping the boat into the jungle. Thankfully, everything went well, and we now had a safer mode of river travel.

Other boat trips, though less dramatic, were still memorable. Sundays were always fun. In the afternoon, we would go on a family trip upriver to visit other Fayu clans. A couple of Iyarike always went with us to help further their relationship with the other clans. The trips lasted several hours, so we entertained ourselves with enthusiastic singing. Our favourite, which I remember to this day, was a German children's song about a coconut. *The monkeys raced through the jungle, knocking each other out cold. As the entire monkey troop yells:* (and then the entire family would chime in on the chorus as loudly as we could) *Where is the coconut? Where is the coconut? Who stole the coconut?* We felt lucky. Most German children never get the opportunity to sing the jungle song while actually in a jungle.

After several rounds of the coconut song, the Fayu would attempt to join in on the chorus. I suspect that the raucous, chaotic scene would probably have looked a bit crazy to an outsider. We, however, enjoyed it thoroughly.

One time, we wanted to visit the Sefoidi clan, who lived the farthest upriver. It was another hot day, and the humidity was getting to us. After several hours of travel, we decided to turn off into a small stream that fed into the

Klihi River. The water there ran clear, and it looked like a perfect spot to swim and cool off.

This turned out to be a great spot for several reasons. Fallen logs spanned the width of the stream, blocking off debris and providing a spot to anchor the boat. Our entire family jumped into the water. Judith used the opportunity to wash her hair. She sat on one of the logs and began to shampoo.

After a while, Papa noticed that none of the Fayu had gotten out of the boat. They simply watched our activities with great interest. Papa held onto the edge of the boat and encouraged the men to jump into the cool water. Nakire shook his head and said that they didn't swim in this river. Concerned that we might be violating some sort of taboo, Papa asked Nakire if this was a sacred river.

'No, no,' Nakire answered. 'This is the Crocodile River where we catch all the crocodiles we eat.' I've never seen anyone climb into a boat as quickly as Papa did at that moment.

'Out! Get out!' Papa shouted. 'Crocodiles!' We quickly followed his example. Poor Judith still had a head full of shampoo but refused to dip her hair into the water even for the two seconds it would require to rinse it.

When we were all safely gathered in the boat, Papa asked the Fayu why they hadn't said anything. They nonchalantly replied, 'Well, because everybody knows this is the Crocodile River.' Once our terror faded, we had to laugh at this typical Fayu attitude – just sitting there, impressed by the fact that we weren't scared. It never occurred to them that our 'bravery' was really ignorance. Needless to say, from that day on we always asked first before jumping into a new river.

As we were heading back to the main river, the Fayu

explained to us that the reason so many crocodiles lived in that stream was that it contained an amazing quantity of large fish. Since the current was weaker, it was an ideal place for the fish to lay their eggs.

That caught our attention! The next week we returned, properly equipped with fishhooks and lines. The Fayu were right – the river was ripe with fish.

We didn't have fishing rods, so we fashioned our own, which consisted of a short, flat piece of wood (about five inches by two inches) into which we had bored a hole. The fishing line was anchored through that centre hole. Then a V shape was cut into both ends of the wood so that the fishing line could be coiled around it. At the end of the line we attached a fishhook and a small stone to serve as the sinker. Voilà! A jungle-style fishing pole!

Next, we needed worms. There were two types that made for excellent bait: fat, white grubs (a decent food source in their own right) and long, dark earthworms. The jungle was full of both, and Christian, Tuare, Bebe, Dihida and I made a game out of who could collect the most.

Back at the river, we would tie the 'fishing poles' to the vegetation that overhung the bank. Every few yards, we would tie another until there was a row of at least ten to fifteen of them. By the time we tied off the last pole, the first one would have a fish on it.

Within an hour we caught more fish than we could eat. Usually these were catfish, which grew to be about a yard long with a weight of ten to fifteen pounds. I realize that this probably sounds like a tall fish tale, but it's the truth – I promise.

Back home in Foida, we would start a large fire. The Fayu built an elevated grill over the coals out of thin, green branches. That evening, the entire village was invited to the fish fry. We sat around eating delicious fish while some of the Fayu warriors acted out exciting hunting stories. It was our version of dinner theatre.

But it was called the Crocodile River for a reason. They were the kings of this river, and one day, they decided to demonstrate this to us. It was during our third or fourth fishing expedition. We had all ready tied off our lines and were coming back to the first one to retrieve the fish. But when Papa pulled up the line, there was nothing there. No fish. No fishhook. The line had been severed.

Before we had time to figure out what had happened, a monstrous crocodile shot vertically out of the water only one or two yards from our boat. Jaws wide open, he propelled nearly his entire body out of the water. We screamed and jumped to the other side of the boat as his body came crashing down in our direction, spraying water all over us. His jaws barely missed the boat. If one of us had had an arm or leg in the water, it would have turned out very badly. We didn't dare move for several minutes, but the crocodile had disappeared.

We had several close encounters of the crocodile kind. The Fayu tried to reassure us by saying that the crocodiles were only marking their territory. We hoped that they were right. Generally speaking, crocodiles aren't overly aggressive unless they are provoked. So we exercised caution whenever we spotted one. We kept our arms and legs out of the water, and we kept our distance.

On a different outing, we discovered the most idyllic spot on earth. Travelling upriver, hot and hungry as usual, we searched the riverbank for a spot to picnic. Among the dense vegetation, we saw a narrow opening just wide enough for the boat. As we entered it, we found ourselves in what looked like a cove with a small stream exiting out the back. The water was shallow here, so we raised the motor and paddled in.

Following the stream out the back side of the cove, we felt as though we had discovered paradise. We were so overcome by the sight that no one said a word. The trees on the riverbank were covered by thousands of red flame orchids. Their vines dropped down into the water, forming a red tapestry from the river to the sky. The water was as clear as crystal and as smooth as a mirror. Brightly coloured birds flitted among the trees, singing their exuberant birdsongs.

This paradise held a special surprise for us children — banks made of soft, grey clay. I had barely left the boat when Christian grabbed a handful and slung it at me. I shrieked and returned the favour. Unfortunately, Christian ducked, and my missile hit Judith in the back. She whipped around and within a few minutes, we were all involved in a grand clayball fight. Partially due to our bad aim, even the Fayu got involved. It was great fun. We often returned to this secret spot, which we called the 'Sunday River'.

20

MY BROTHER OHRI

My heart melted when I saw Ohri for the first time. He was about eight years old and lame. He got around by pulling himself along the ground with his arms. Ohri was skinny and weak, his crooked legs reduced to nothing but skin and bones. His parents had been killed in front of his eyes during one of the many tribal wars. Now he lived with another family from his clan.

We took him in, gave him food to eat and started spending a lot of time with him. As the years went by, he became like a brother to us kids and a son to Mama and Papa, although he didn't actually live with us. At the beginning, he followed Mama around everywhere, not wanting to leave her side. As his nutrition improved, Ohri became stronger and learned to walk with the help of crutches. First he learned to stand and then hobble as we looked on with delight. It seemed like a miracle.

Then one day, on our return from Danau Bira, he stood

up. With a proud grin he walked toward us without crutches. We were overwhelmed with joy for him.

A year later, as I was building a fire with Christian, Ohri came out of the jungle. We had been worried about him, as we had not seen him for some time. This was not especially unusual, since the Fayu are a nomadic people who live a hunter-gatherer existence. They only came to Foida when we were there. Otherwise they followed their usual pattern of moving from hut to hut. Each family within a clan had several square miles in which they built three to four huts. They lived in each hut for three to four months as they hunted and gathered food in that area. When the edible plants and prey became scarce, they would move on to the next hut. By the time the family cycled through all of its huts, a year had passed and the territory surrounding the first one would be restocked.

Each time we returned to Foida, the pilot would fly a circle over the Fayu territory, letting them know we had returned. Then those who wanted to would return to the village. This process could take a week or two, so we hoped that Ohri's absence was simply due to the distance he had to travel to get back to Foida.

But this time our concern was justified. When I saw Ohri step out of the brush, I shouted for Mama and hurried to him. He collapsed to the ground, weak and with a high fever. I wanted to help him up but didn't know where I could touch him. His entire chest was a huge, infected wound covered by a thick layer of green-grey fungus. The Fayu had shot him with an arrow and left him for dead in the middle of the jungle.

Mama came running and helped Ohri into our house. Papa asked the Fayu what had happened and was told that Ohri had eaten a forbidden piece of a crocodile. This was his punishment. They completely ignored him and acted as though he didn't exist any more.

I started to cry when I saw his pain-streaked face. He smelled like rotting meat. The wound was obviously gangrenous. I sat next to him and held his hand. Mama brought bandages and medication and rolled Ohri on to his side. She mixed potassium permanganate with water and poured it over his chest. An inch-thick fungal growth slowly loosened itself and fell off him onto the leaves we had placed underneath him.

Ohri was in great pain. His entire chest was an open wound filled with maggots. Mama cut a bedsheet into large strips, covered them in antibiotic cream, and bound his torso with them. She changed the bandages every day. Papa took the leaves and dressings out behind the house and burned them.

'Mama, is he going to die?' I kept asking through my tears.

'I don't know,' Mama replied. 'We'll do everything we can to save him.'

I helped to care for Ohri's wounds as much as I could. We fed him, and he slept in our house, where he spent his days watching us do schoolwork. When we were finished, we listened to cassettes with him and showed him our picture books. The fever broke within a couple of days, and in the following weeks, the wound miraculously healed, leaving behind an enormous scar. Mother confessed to me afterward that she had not believed that Ohri would survive. But survive he did, and he was soon playing with us again as if nothing had happened.

Ohri grew up with us and soon was taller than me. We loved him because of his wonderful personality. He was a gentle creature, full of love. I never saw him angry or unpleasant. He became an important part of my life.

21

BAT WINGS AND
GRILLED WORMS

At some point, a friend from America sent us a poster of a large bowl of ice cream. Mama hung it on the wall next to our table, where we kids sat and admired it. I still remember the picture very clearly. In it was a large silver bowl filled with fifteen or sixteen scoops of ice cream, each a different flavour. It was crowned with a mountain of whipped cream whose peak was a red cherry.

How often we sat in the oppressive heat and dreamed of this ice cream! We spent hours staring at the poster, trying to guess the various flavours. Occasionally, Mama would help, but usually we would just use our imagination. The white scoop was *sago* ice cream, the orange one was mango, and the yellow one must be made from sweet potatoes. None of us could remember the taste of ice cream, but it looked so good. We were convinced that it must be the best food in the world.

Years later, when we visited Jakarta, the capital of Indonesia, what we looked forward to the most was eating ice cream. Mama had all ready made some inquiries and found that there actually was an ice cream parlour in the city. We wanted to go the moment our plane touched down and were very disappointed when Mama told us that the café was closed at that late hour. We weren't quite sure whether to believe her, but she promised to take us the next day.

The next morning rolled around, and then it was time – the day of the great ice cream, as we called it. We entered the café with crazed excitement. So much ice cream in one place was simply overwhelming, especially when the only ice cream we'd ever seen was on a poster in the jungle. My parents, who were watching us with amusement, ordered the largest ice cream creation the store offered. It was called 'The Earthquake'. This monstrosity contained fifteen scoops of ice cream in a variety of colours and flavours. We were in heaven. One of our biggest dreams was being fulfilled, and it tasted as good as we had imagined it would. I still remember how oddly important and satisfying this moment was. Even Mama and Papa joined in with enthusiasm.

When we had finished the first Earthquake, we begged for more. Mama warned us that we would get sick but left the choice up to us. We promptly ignored her and ate another bowl of ice cream anyway.

As it turned out, Mama was right. When we returned to the hotel that afternoon, we promptly began a vomiting session that lasted throughout the day and kept us all in bed. Our stomachs simply weren't used to the cold, let alone the excessive amount of sugar and dairy. This was such an extreme contrast to our usual jungle diet.

There is a very limited selection of food in the jungle. As a result, our diet did not vary much from day to day: pork, fish, sago (the heart of a swamp palm), rice, sweet potatoes, cornflakes with milk powder, kwa (breadfruit), occasionally eggs and *kasbi* (a tree root that tastes like potatoes). It sounds like a lot of variety until you consider that these were the *only* choices, meal after meal, day after day, year after year. We tried planting various kinds of squash, but between the flooding and the boars' voracious appetites, it was never a reliable source of food for us. But as children, we didn't know anything else, and we couldn't miss what we didn't know.

What we ate most frequently was kwa. We had a bread-fruit tree next to our house, so whenever we were hungry, one of the Fayu climbed the tree and cut some down for us. Kwa trees are rather large and the fruit grows at the ends of the branches. Harvesting them required us to not only climb the tree but also to use a twenty-foot pole that had a knife tied to the tip. Our part was to gather up the fruit that was harvested and lay it in the fire until it blackened on the outside. Then we plucked it out, and one of the Fayu stomped on it with bare feet.

I admired this skill and really wanted to be able to do it myself. Unfortunately, I didn't take into consideration that my feet were not nearly as calloused as those of the Fayu. So when I stomped down on the fruit, I felt a terrible burning sensation. I began to scream and started hopping on the other foot. Christian found this hilarious and could barely stop laughing. Mama just gave me a lecture on the perils of disobedience and my lack of common sense.

The burns on the sole of my foot caused me to hobble around for days. It was a long time before I dared try to open a kwa with my foot again. This time it went better, since by then my feet were more calloused and up to the task.

Sago was the primary staple food for the Fayu. Its preparation involved heavy physical labour, which was carried out by the women of the village. First, they split open the sago palm. Then, they scraped out the centre of it and mixed it with water so that it turned into a sticky white mass resembling a flour paste. After they cooked it in a fire, they ate it plain or with a filling of cooked meat.

Some of our favourite foods, crocodile and snake meat, were harder to obtain. One evening, the Fayu brought us two large snakes. They claimed that they were delicious, so Papa traded something for them. The Fayu were quite right – it was delicious white meat, tender and sweet. It's still the best meat I've ever eaten.

Whenever the Fayu went on a crocodile-hunting expedition, we waited in great anticipation for their return. Crocodile meat is prepared in the same manner as meat from a wild boar, ostrich, tree kangaroo or fish. A wooden grill is built over the top of the fire, and the meat is slowly smoked on it. We would trade for the tail of the crocodile, which was second only to snake meat in taste.

When I returned to Europe years later, it took a long time before I could eat the meat there. It tasted old and bitter. Judith never got used to the taste of it and even had an allergic reaction, so she ended up becoming a vegetarian.

In the evenings after the crocodile feasts, we sat around the fire, watching the colourful sunsets paint the dimming sky. Insects and birds sang their evening songs. The air was filled with a mixture of smoke and the sweet perfumes of the jungle. And then, in this magical atmosphere, the stories would begin – stories of the hunt.

The great thing about the stories is that they weren't just recounted with words but were acted out by the warriors, one of whom played the part of the prey. I listened and watched intently. Perhaps the reason I love the theatre so much today is because it brings back these memories.

The Fayu's hunting technique made for great storytelling. First, they wove long ropes from the bark of trees. Outfitted with the ropes and stone axes, they would paddle up to Crocodile River. At midday, when the sun was directly overhead, the warriors would climb ashore and then send the youngest hunter into the water. The water there was so clear that the noonday sun shone all the way to the bottom of the riverbed.

The young hunter would swim along the surface, carrying three ropes, until he saw the shadow of a crocodile at the bottom of the river. He would then dive and very carefully approach the beast from the back, then swim to the front in order to see if his eyes were open or closed. If they were open, the hunter would withdraw as quickly as possible. If the eyes were closed, the man would place a looped rope around the crocodile's mouth and one around each of its front legs. He would then bring the free end of the ropes to the warriors waiting on the bank. As a group, they would drag the crocodile onto land and beat it on the neck with their stone axes until it was dead.

The first thing they did after killing a crocodile was cut open its belly. A crocodile has two stomachs, one of which is used to collect the gravel and debris that is swallowed when it scoops up prey. This stomach was cut out and quickly buried, as it was considered a taboo part of the animal. The Fayu believed that if a woman saw it, she would get sick and die. The crocodile would then be loaded into the canoe and brought back to the village and shared with the others.

The Fayu's crocodile-hunting method was obviously dangerous. Wrestling a crocodile tends to put you inches from the massive jaws, which are only restrained by a single rope. Today, the Fayu use metal spear tips and machetes that they gained from us in trade. These items reduce some of the dangers.

Everyone enjoyed the crocodile feast, in part because it happened so rarely. Generally speaking, our menus did not include such delicacies. So for the sake of variation, we children would try everything the Fayu ate.

The huge red ants were quite popular and easy to find. We would grab them by the head and bite off their bodies. It was quite important not to eat the head, which I didn't discover until one bit me on the tongue. Judith teased me because I couldn't speak properly for a while. Jungle food has to be eaten with caution – it can bite back.

Another local favourite was the bat – especially the large fruit bats whose wingspan could reach up to five feet or so. They spent their days sleeping in clusters on trees and at night ate any and all fruit they could find. This diet made the meat tender and tasty. The sleeping habits made them easy prey.

We would usually cook the entire bat over the fire. The Fayu, on the other hand, liked to lay only the body between layers of sago, sort of like a hamburger. The whole thing would be wrapped in large leaves and laid in the fire.

Grilled bat wings are nice and crispy. But we also had the brilliant idea of trying them raw. They felt rather rubbery, and we thought they might make good chewing gum. So we washed them, cut them up into little pieces, and popped them into our mouths. Sadly, it didn't taste quite as good as we had hoped.

Ever-present grubs were another tasty alternative. The best were the fat, white ones that we used as fish bait. We speared them with small arrows and then browned them over the fire.

I remember one time when Nakire's wife, Fusai, brought some sago to eat with our grubs. We helped her pack the grubs into the sago and put it on the fire. We could hardly wait for it to be ready. I was allowed to have the first taste. I opened my mouth as wide as I could and took a huge bite. When I looked closer, however, I noticed that the inside wasn't fully cooked. The worms were still alive. In the same moment I saw one poke its head out of the sago, I felt movement in my mouth.

I didn't want to insult Fusai, so I bravely swallowed. But this was my limit. According to the custom, I passed the food on to the next person. When it was my turn again, I just nibbled at the crust. Tuare, sitting next to me, appreciated my restraint and ate both our portions with great delight.

We didn't eat just meat and insects. The jungle had far more to offer. Every five years, the lychee tree would bear fruit. And for several weeks, we would eat nothing else. Lychee fruit is red and covered in spikes; the whole thing is the size of a golf ball. We peeled off the skin and ate the pulp surrounding the large seed. We then spat the seeds onto the ground, where the boars later enjoyed them. A perfect recycling system.

Perhaps our favourite plant was sugarcane. Mama always tried to keep us away from it and never tired of reminding us that it was bad for our teeth. One day, however, we found a large clump of it growing on the riverbank. After cutting it down, we peeled the hard skin with our teeth and chewed on the stringy interior. For several weeks after our discovery, it seemed like the entire ground around our house was covered with sugarcane peelings.

Eventually this was too much for Mama, and she forbid us the sugary goodness. We paid earnest attention as she lectured us. Everybody nodded in agreement as she explained that our teeth would turn black and fall out if we kept eating it. And as soon as she went back into the house, we ran to the village, found a good hiding place and ate as much sugarcane as we possibly could. The ground around our house stayed clean, but it was best that Mama didn't look behind the huts of the Fayu village.

Occasionally the helicopter would come bringing tastes from the outside world. I remember one time when the pilot brought us a thermos full of ice cubes. We were delighted. Mama gave us each an equal portion on plates. We immediately went outside to show them to our friends. When Christian placed one into Dihida's hand, Dihida cried out, 'It burned me!' and dropped it. He had never felt anything so cold and mistook the sensation for heat.

What really fascinated the Fayu was how the ice slowly disappeared. We had a great time watching the brave warriors shriek like children as they competed to see who could hold an ice cube the longest without dropping it. Even the reserved Chief Baou had to investigate this new phenomenon.

The pilot had also brought us some raisins. His wife had received a package of them from America – just our luck, she didn't like them. Mama, however, loved raisins and immediately made pancakes filled with them, which she shared with the Fayu women.

When she checked later to see how they liked the pancakes, Mama noticed all the raisins lying on the ground, being eaten by the dingoes and piglets, who were really enjoying them. A surprised Mama asked the women why they had picked out the best part. The women politely responded that they preferred not to eat bugs they didn't know. After all, they could be poisonous. But the rest tasted quite good – thank you very much.

We all laughed when we heard this explanation, but Mama did mourn for her nice raisins.

22

THE FAYU LANGUAGE

We learned as young children that people speak in different languages. Since we grew up in foreign countries, we had to learn a number of languages: Nepalese, Danuwar Rai, German, English, Indonesian and eventually Fayu. This created a bit of confusion in our household.

Our schooling was in English, and we had a fair number of English books. Some days, especially during the rainy season, there was nothing to do but sit around the house. The rain would thunder down onto the aluminium roof with such force that normal conversation was impossible. So we all learned to read quite early in life, and before long, we had gone through all of our available books.

To keep our German skills alive, Mama would read to us from German books, as we had not yet learned to read German for ourselves. We would sit with her in bed as she read us popular children's books like *Hanni and Nanni* and *Am Samstag kam das Sams zurück*. Friends of ours also sent us copies of the comics *Asterix and Obelix* and *Tintin*. I learned to read German from these.

This was a lengthy process. As most of the other foreign kids spoke English, we children increasingly spoke English among ourselves, to our parents' mild dismay. As our German became corrupted, we began speaking in a mixture of languages. For example, a typical sentence might sound something like 'Judith, come here, I want to *zeigen dir was!*' So my parents began to insist that we speak German in the house.

When I listen to the tape recordings my parents made of us, I can hear a strong American flavour to our German. To this day, I am frequently told that I speak German with a slight accent.

Over time, we also began to learn the Fayu language. When we first arrived among the Fayu, Christian had a fair bit of difficulty. We spoke fluent Indonesian, and he couldn't understand why the Fayu didn't respond to it. Papa explained that they spoke a completely different language even though they lived in Indonesia. And so we prepared ourselves to start all over again. We went around pointing at objects and tried to remember the words they told us.

One of the first words we learned was *di*, which means 'water'. Testing my skills, I once said to Tuare, '*Di*, Tuare', in the hope that he would bring me some water. We had just lit a fire, and I wanted to cook some soup. But when Tuare came back, he handed me a knife.

'*Hau*, Tuare, *di!*' (No, Tuare, water!) I said gruffly.

He looked at me with some confusion and then walked away. It took quite a while before he returned. To my big surprise, he appeared with a piglet under his arm, which he handed to me. Now totally confused, I stared at the squealing piglet that was wriggling like crazy in my arms. I looked back at Tuare. Clearly, I was missing something. I let the piglet go, took Tuare by the hand, and went in search of Papa.

When he heard the story, Papa broke out in laughter. That just frustrated me even more. So Papa sat me on his lap and explained that the Fayu language was a tonal language.

'What does that mean?' I asked in confusion.

He explained that in a tonal language, the same words mean different things depending on the pitch with which they're said. Papa used my present situation to explain.

'When you told Tuare to get you *di*, you must have said it using a middle pitch, so he got you a knife. Then you used a deeper voice to say *di*, so he brought you a piglet. If you mean water, you have to say *di* in a high tone.'

I turned to Tuare, and in the highest tones I could achieve, I squeaked, '*Di*, Tuare!' He grinned at me, and in a flash I had my water.

So now we didn't just have to learn new words but also a variety of tones. To explain, the Fayu language uses three different pitches – a high tone, which in writing is notated by /1/, a middle tone (/2/) and a low tone (/3/). For example:

Di /1/ means 'water'

Di /2/ means 'knife'

Di /3/ means 'boar'

Additionally, there are two tone combinations – a high to low progression within the same word (denoted by /1-3/) and a middle to low progression (/2-3/). Examples of this would be:

Fu /1/, which means 'canoe', and

Fu /1-3/, which means 'log'

Kui /3/, which means 'grandfather', and

Kui /1-3/, which means 'message'

This obviously makes linguistic study more challenging. Sentences written out with phonetic notation end up looking like this:

A /3/ tai /2-3/ da /2/ re /3/ means 'I've eaten egg'.

A /3/ fe /2/ ri /2/ ba /2/ ri /3/ means 'I saw fish'.

De /3/ boi /3/ da /2/ re /3/ means 'You ate yesterday'.

The Fayu vocabulary is very limited. Most of their words relate to the jungle and indicate plants, animals or activities. For example, there are no specific words for 'sorry', 'thank you', or 'hello'. They do have a word that could mean any of the above, plus a few other things: *asahaego*. This could alternately mean 'good morning', 'okay', 'thank you', 'goodbye' and anything else that had no specific word.

Some words were straightforward, of course. *Bau* means 'yes'; *hau* means 'no'. *Kaha* is 'good'; *fay* is 'bad'. But generally speaking, a phrase often has several possible meanings, depending on the context in which it is used. So *Sabine awaru kaha* literally means 'Sabine's heart is good'. But this could also mean 'I (Sabine) am doing well', 'I am happy', or 'I am a good person and haven't done anything wrong'.

And to further complicate things, all words have to end in a vowel sound. This is how my mother, Doris, became Doriso, and Klaus became Klausu. Due to all of these intricacies, it takes twenty to thirty years on average to completely analyse a tonal language. It took years of meticulous work for my father to assemble a Fayu dictionary.

As kids we didn't concern ourselves with these details. If our friends couldn't understand something, we would use our hands and feet to explain it. If we came across something for which the Fayu didn't have a word, we simply taught them the Indonesian word for it. Problem solved.

23

TARZAN AND JANE

One day Christian came running to me in great excitement. He said that he had found the coolest thing. His eyes beamed and a proud grin covered his face. I looked at him skeptically. Our world in the jungle had very narrow geographic limits. It extended from the Klihi River to the edge of the underbrush and down to the Fayu village. What could he have found that I didn't know about all ready?

I followed Christian and saw with astonishment that he was making a beeline toward the jungle. At the edge of the brush, he glanced back toward the house to make sure no one was watching. Mama and Papa had never expressly forbidden us to go into the jungle, but it was an unwritten rule that we had instinctively obeyed for years. The jungle was simply too dangerous a place for young children alone. But this day, we ignored it. With a prickling sensation, I followed Christian into the unexplored depths.

I loved the thick, secretive, ancient forest that stretched

above me. There was something magical about crossing from the clearing around our home into the shadowy dominion of the rain forest. It was like stepping into another world. Outside, where the sun was burning down on me, the temperature reached over one hundred degrees, with humidity of over ninety percent. But here in the shade of the trees, cooler air descended on me. I was covered in its secretive quiet, with only the muted sounds of insects here and there.

This air even smelled different than the air outside the forest. It was sweeter, filled with aromas that floated out of the exotic flowers and plants. The sweetness of the air was periodically punctuated by the sharp smell of rotting vegetation and the distinctive odour of a swamp. Oddly, it was not an unpleasant smell. The dank odours mixed with the sweet ones like harmonic counterpoints in a finely tuned orchestra.

I looked around and could see nothing but green. There were various ferns surrounding my feet. Young trees poked their heads up among the ferns, straining to reach the light rays far above. But they were dwarfed by the giant trees around them, which towered so high above me that I could not see their tips. These massive creatures had enormous root systems that arched out of the floor of the jungle – almost like prehistoric earthworms. It was an unforgettable scene.

Christian's voice drew me out of my reverie. He showed me a small path he had found – one likely forged by wild boars. As we followed the curvy trail, I felt as though we were being watched. The plants themselves seemed to want to grab us. I got a funny feeling in the pit of my stomach as I remembered how easy it was to get lost in the jungle.

So I stayed close to Christian, who gave the impression that he knew his way around. After several minutes, I saw bright lights among the ferns up ahead. A few rays of sunlight found their way to the dark earthen floor. And suddenly, the dense underbrush was interrupted by a clearing. I stood there open-mouthed and wondered at it.

In Foida, we lived at the edge of a swamp not too far from a small mountain chain. There were hills and valleys randomly scattered about, and that was what lay before us now. The ground undulated, producing a small, elevated plateau.

But that wasn't what captured my eyes. Rather, it was something I had seen only once before, in Danau Bira. Hanging from the trees that stretched to the heavens were hundreds of thick, brown vines. They were attached so high up in the trees that we could not see where they originated. Christian and I looked at each other, big grins covering our dirty faces. We had always been convinced that we were distant cousins of Tarzan, and now finally there was opportunity to prove it.

We clambered up the small hill with great enthusiasm. I grabbed a vine and with a cry that would have put Tarzan to shame, I swung down the hill. The wind whipped through my hair as the green blurred around me. For a second, I was suspended in the air before beginning to swing back on the return flight. It is amazing how far one can travel on a vine.

After this successful trial run, I released the vine and stood again on solid ground. It was Christian's turn next. He got a running start and managed to swing even farther than me. Now experienced vine swingers, we decided to go airborne at the same time. I chose one of the many other vines that seemed to be just waiting for a passenger. Then I discovered something that Tarzan probably didn't know. Not all vines are firmly attached to their tree.

I grabbed the vine and backpedalled as far as I could. Racing toward the edge of the plateau, I jumped into the air. Shortly thereafter, there was a horrible ripping sound as the vine released its grip on the tree. I crashed deep into the underbrush.

There was a moment of silence, and then I heard Christian's gloating laughter. I stood up, covered from top to bottom in mud. Leaves and grass stuck out of my blond hair. Even I had to laugh. After a quick check for injuries, I climbed back up the hill to try again.

This time I carefully checked the vine's rip factor before Christian and I decided to try a tandem swing. First we had an extensive discussion as to who would be Tarzan and who would be Jane. We both wanted to be Tarzan, but Christian insisted that as a girl, I logically had to be Jane. I retorted that it would be silly for Jane to be bigger than Tarzan, and as the older sibling, I naturally had the right to claim that honour. In the end, we decided to change the story. I was Tarzan, and Christian was the long-lost brother of Tarzan whom they had simply forgotten to mention in the story.

We grabbed a thick vine and jumped off. Sadly, despite all precautions, this vine didn't hold either, and we landed, laughing, on our backsides. Now we were both covered in dirt, but still unscathed. If someone had seen us at that moment, they would have mistaken us for natives.

Just as we were climbing the hill for another attempt, a figure came out of the jungle. It was Nakire, coming to take us home. The Fayu had tattled. But we were too happy to let that bother us. It had been a great experience.

Because of this day, the formerly unspoken rule about not

entering the jungle without permission from both parents now became an expressed law – one that we obeyed because we recognized that the jungle could be a dangerous place, even if it was the next best thing to an amusement park.

24

ANIMAL COLLECTION, PART TWO

The Fayu were constantly amused that they could go to the white folks and trade all sorts of animals for knives or fishhooks. That the white folks sometimes released the animals afterward was even more amusing.

A Fayu who had recently returned from hunting brought me a small parrot. I immediately fell in love and had to have it. But there was a problem, namely that Mama had recently told me, 'Sabine, I've about had it with your collection. It's big enough.' My favourite bat had died, and I buried it in a dramatic show of tears. Then I naturally began to inquire about getting a replacement. It was at this point that Mama began laying down the law. But this parrot was so cute, I thought that even Mama couldn't resist its charms. Sadly, I was mistaken.

'No! No! No!' she said with determination. 'No more animals!' And of course, it was that very morning that Judith's tree kangaroo, Fifi, had left a small 'present' in Mama's bed. But that wasn't *my* fault! My tears flowed, but Mama remained stalwart. Crying never worked with her.

Dejected, I sat outside on the stairs with the parrot on my arm. I had all ready named him Bobby. He stood there watching me with big, curious eyes and shared my pain. Christian brought some breadfruit, which Bobby ate, to our great delight. And then it was time to let Bobby go free.

'Life is hard,' my mother said without pity, and turned to go back into the house. I glared at her back and with heavy heart untied the string from Bobby's leg. I sat him on a nearby branch, and when he took off, I broke down in tears again. The day was ruined. Life was unfair. And losing such a pretty parrot was a profound tragedy.

The next morning, I woke up early and went outside to find some breadfruit for breakfast. I sat down on the stairs and began to eat when I heard a quiet fluttering next to me. There was Bobby, greedily looking at my breakfast. I could barely believe my luck! Bobby had returned to me of his own free will, without a string and without Mama's permission. This was the beginning of my long friendship with the strange and smart little bird.

Bobby stayed around the house, and I fed him. He amused us in his funny little way, even learning to speak a couple of words after a while. Mother turned a blind eye to the relationship, since he wasn't technically a pet. But it seemed as if Bobby knew that Mama had voted against him in the beginning, and he went out of his way to annoy her.

It began one day with the laundry. Mama washed our clothing once or twice a week in the river. Then she hung it out to dry on the clothesline behind the house. Bobby liked sitting on the clothesline, which Mama didn't mind. But one day we heard her angrily calling out, 'Who did this?'

Curious, we ran behind the house. The entire load of laundry that Mama had hung up that morning was laying on the ground, clothespegs scattered about. As always, Mama looked at me first. 'Sabine,' she said sternly. 'How could you?'

I shook my head indignantly. 'I would never do that!' And for once, I meant it. Nobody would confess to the deed, and Mama had no choice but to wash everything again.

A few days later, the same thing happened. But this time, Mama was more alert and she caught the scoundrel red-handed. It was Bobby, who happily plucked at the clothespegs and spat them onto the ground. Mama was furious, but Bobby was too quick for her. He gave *her* a stern lecture from high up in the tree.

Their next confrontation occurred during her afternoon nap. Mama would often lie down during the hottest part of the day, and we knew not to disturb her. But Bobby had a different idea. He seemed to take great delight in sitting outside her window, screeching as loudly as he could. By the time Mama ran outside, he was always gone.

She tolerated this for a few weeks before deciding to show Bobby who was boss. Before laying down for her nap, she filled a bucket with water and placed it by the window. The innocent Bobby had barely begun his midday concert when Mama threw the entire bucketful on his head. The afternoon nap had been saved. At least till the next time.

One day, this didn't go so smoothly. As always, Mama's fully loaded bucket was ready by the window. She lay down and waited for Bobby to begin his screeching. At his first note, she ran to the bucket and tossed its contents out the window. But this time there was a chorus of loud yelling instead of the expected wet squawking. Mama looked out the window in surprised dismay. Directly underneath the window, Papa was sitting with a Fayu warrior who had come upriver to trade.

Papa ran into the house and yelled, 'What were you thinking? Don't you know that he is one of the most dangerous warriors?'

Mama had startled herself but didn't let Papa know it. Coolly, she said, 'And how should I know that? Is he wearing a sign that says, "I am a dangerous warrior. Don't pour water over my head"? And besides, I didn't see you. I was concentrating on the parrot.'

Somewhat mollified, Papa said, 'Well, you need to apologize. Figure out a way to do that.' He went back outside to the Fayu warrior, who was still quite upset.

I looked nervously at Mama and whispered, 'Oh Mama, what are you going to do now?'

'You will see,' she answered, collecting up Papa's big bath towel and several other items. Mama went outside, still angry that Papa had yelled at her.

The warrior had moved to a campfire and looked up at Mama with annoyance. She brought her hands together in a clapping motion and bowed several times. Mama had often seen Fayu do this when they wanted to apologize to one another. Then she took Papa's towel and dried the warrior's head. He was placated and left with the towel, along with the other items Mama had brought. Papa wasn't really happy about this but there wasn't much he could do.

'Well,' Mama said dryly, 'that would be the end of your towel.' We thoroughly enjoyed seeing the look on Papa's face as she turned around and walked back to the house.

Years later, when Bobby disappeared into the jungle and didn't come back, even Mama mourned for him.

CHAPTER THE ELEVENTH

25

MALARIA AND OTHER DISEASES

When I tell people about growing up in the jungle, they often ask me – especially if they are parents themselves – how we made do without doctors and hospitals. As children, we never really thought about it, and my parents relied upon their faith.

In the West, children often struggle with colds, stuffy noses, coughs and other annoyances. In the jungle, we didn't get colds. Instead, malaria became our constant companion. The mosquitoes were as numerous as grains of sand on a beach. We had almost got used to the itchy bites and didn't really take notice of them any more. But eventually you'd get bitten by the wrong one and end up with 'The Disease'.

Malaria doesn't develop gradually but rather attacks you all at once. You wake up in the morning feeling fine, eat your breakfast as usual and go about your business. Then suddenly you feel dizzy. Your legs buckle and the urge to vomit sets in. A high fever follows within several minutes. Your whole body seems to burn, and you strip out of your clothes in an attempt to cool down. Nothing can stop the heat, and you find yourself wishing to be packed in ice.

When someone places a cool, wet washcloth on your head, it seems to help for a moment. The heat relents a little, and you feel cooler. But then the temperature starts to go further down. You get bitterly cold; your entire body shivers. So you put on a sweatshirt and some long pants and crawl under a thick blanket, but nothing helps. It is freezing. So you get a hot water bottle, which helps a little bit. But the water isn't hot enough – never hot enough. You add another blanket. It doesn't help.

Then finally some warmth comes back into your body. You get hotter and hotter. Blankets get thrown off, clothing too. You start sweating. Where is that cool washcloth? Your body is burning up. Headaches. Vomiting. Nothing stays down.

Sometimes you hallucinate. Sometimes you lie there too weak to move, convinced that death is around the corner. But eventually things get better. After a few days, the medication kicks in, your temperature stabilizes, your appetite returns, your headaches fade. The malaria has pulled back and is slumbering until the next outbreak.

My first memory of malaria is also my most dramatic one. We were playing as usual when Christian suddenly said that he didn't feel well. Half an hour later, he was lying in bed with malaria. Mama took care of him as Judith and I continued to play. Late that afternoon, Judith turned pale, and minutes later she was in bed . . . malaria.

Papa and I ate supper together and got ready for bed. Mama ran back and forth between Judith and Christian, who were alternately freezing and frying. Judith hallucinated; Christian vomited. Papa slept in Judith's bed so Christian and Judith could sleep with Mama.

It was late before I fell asleep, but after only a couple of hours Mama woke me up. She needed my help. Papa was lying in Judith's bed, surrounded by blankets and jackets. Mama didn't have to explain.

We took care of the others, but I soon noticed that Mama's movements were getting slower and heavier. She was taking longer pauses, bracing herself against the wall. 'Is everything alright?' I asked.

'I'm fine,' Mama answered. But it was easy to tell that this wasn't true. She was sweating heavily. As it slowly became light outside, I began to get seriously worried. Then Mama collapsed, at the end of her strength, her entire body awash with shivering. Now I was completely alone. I ran back and forth between the beds, got cold washcloths and all the blankets I could find, emptied buckets, and brought them back.

A little bit later, it hit me too. I dragged myself over to Papa, told him I didn't feel well, and managed to collapse on a bed. A few hours later, Papa was able to drag himself to the shortwave radio and call to Danau Bira for help. Within half an hour, the helicopter (which, thank God, was working at the time) was on its way to get us. Back in our house at Danau Bira, we received proper care from friends and neighbours.

The others slowly recovered, but something was wrong with me. I kept getting sicker, and the fever didn't want to break. I begged for a warm water bottle. Mama wrapped one in a towel and placed it on my chest. It wasn't hot enough for me, so when she left the room, I removed the towel. About half an hour later, Mama came in to check on me. She saw the towel laying next to me and with a horrified gasp tore the blankets off my body and pulled the hot water bottle away. It was too late. I had extensive burns on my chest, but I was so cold I hadn't noticed it.

An American nurse examined me and whispered something to Papa. He got tears in his eyes, then kneeled down beside my bed and prayed. I couldn't make sense of any of this, and shortly thereafter, everything went dark.

When I woke up again, I felt something hard underneath me. My head was lying on a stone. I was in a dark valley with lights in the distance.

'Mama, the bed is so hard. Please bring me a pillow,' I shouted with all of my strength. It came out as a weak whisper.

I heard Mama answering from a great distance. 'But dear, you have a soft pillow.'

'Please, Mama, help me. Come here,' I whispered with desperation.

'I am here. I am here,' Mama kept repeating. She must have felt at least as desperate as I did. Then everything went dark again.

Papa and Mama stood next to my bed, holding hands and crying. The nurse had told them that she couldn't do anything for me and that this night would decide whether I would live or die. But it wasn't my time to go. When I woke up the next morning, the sun was shining and I had the appetite of a bear.

It wasn't until much later that Mama told me I had almost died. She and Papa had stayed up the whole night with me, praying.

As it turned out, malaria wasn't the only thing that had hit us. Apparently, we had also contracted some unknown virus that weakened our immune systems. This is how the malaria was able to affect us all at the same time.

We got malaria often over the years. Even hepatitis paid me a visit. But the malaria attacks did decrease over time, as our bodies seemed to develop some resistance. I haven't had malaria since returning to Europe. From a medical stand-point, I am now clear.

Infection was the thing we struggled with even more fre-quently than malaria. Sometimes a simple mosquito bite or small scratch was enough to cause a problem. Painful infec-tions could develop overnight, and it would take days to bring them under control. Thankfully, our lives were never endangered by infection, but it was a constant annoyance.

When we were young, Mama would check us every night for scratches. As we got older, we assumed that duty for ourselves, but we weren't as conscientious as Mama might have been. Of course, we would pay for it the next day with an infection that had to be dressed every few hours.

One time, for example, I woke up with a pain on my knee but ignored it. A new day full of adventure was wait-ing for me, and I wouldn't let myself be distracted by minor pain. I jumped out of bed, ate breakfast, finished my school-work as quickly as my inattentive brain would allow, and ran out to play. But the pain kept getting worse. After a while, it felt like my knee was throbbing as though it had been hit by a hammer.

When I couldn't run any more, I hobbled to Mama, who told me to wait a second. I sat down on the wooden bench in the kitchen and inspected what looked like an infected mosquito bite. The infection seemed to be visibly worsening. The most interesting part of this was the five red lines spreading out in various directions from the bite. *Fascinating,* I thought, and continued to watch.

When Mama came to check on me a short while later, she reacted with worried surprise. She told me to lie down immediately and explained that I had blood poisoning. This would be very dangerous if the red lines reached my heart. Mama made it sound dramatic, but I didn't pay it that much attention. After all, the red lines were slower than snails, and I was getting bored laying in bed. Thanks to Mama's ministrations and a few antibiotics, I was soon able to get back to playing.

Generally speaking, I was almost criminally careless about my own health. Even deep wounds didn't impress me. I accidentally cut myself deeply several times with a knife, only to make superficial attempts at cleaning and bandaging. I was always more concerned with getting back to whatever game we were playing at the moment.

I rarely wore shoes, but since it took a while to develop good calluses, I wounded myself a lot in the beginning. As a result, I had almost constant infections around my toes. Mama became quite frustrated with me running around with dirty bandages on my feet when I was supposed to be wearing shoes to cover them. I didn't care. I was too busy to worry about it.

So one day, Mama told me earnestly that all of my toes would fall off if I kept doing this and I would be maimed for life. But why should that bother me? Who would see me beside the Fayu? And they had plenty of their own wounds and scars. On the contrary, I had no problem with scars and maybe some missing toes. Then I could come up with an exciting story about how a crocodile bit them off.

What really worried me however, was ringworm, a type of fungal growth that can spread over the entire body. The Fayu women seemed more susceptible to it than the men, which added to my concern. It didn't take long before I found a red spot on my arm that itched, despite the fact that there was no obvious bite mark. The next morning, I examined it more closely and recognized the distinctive red colouring. I ran crying to Mama, thinking that I would be disfigured for ever. And even worse, ringworm was boring and wouldn't make for a good story. Besides, it itched like crazy. Mama calmed me down and began applying a cream each morning and evening until it went away. I was very relieved.

Whatever disease we contracted, whatever happened to us, Mama could be counted on to find a solution. Our trust in her accompanied us throughout our childhood in the jungle. And my mother did her utmost to also share her knowledge with the Fayu.

26

LEARNING
FORGIVENESS

We had once again received a delicious piece of crocodile tail. Papa had traded a pot for it. It was being smoked in typical fashion over the fire behind our house. Though the process would take a few more hours, we were all ready drooling in anticipation.

Mama was in the back of the house and happened to glance out the window. As she looked down at the meat cooking over the fire, she noticed the young son of Chief Baou. Isori stepped out of the tree cover, cautiously looked around, and crept over to the fire. Apparently, he didn't notice Mama watching from behind the window screen. Grabbing a large piece of meat, he turned to run.

'Hey!' Mama cried out in protest. Isori looked around in great surprise, quickly put the meat back, and ran into the jungle.

In no time at all, everyone knew about the attempted theft. We could hear Chief Baou's angry yells from over three hundred yards away. According to Fayu custom, Papa

Helicopter landing in Foida

A decorated Fayu warrior

Fayu from the Iyareki clan coming to visit us

Doing my schoolwork under the watchful eye of Mama

Papa on his second expedition

Judith with her pet kangaroo Fifi

Papa learning the
Fayu language

Papa rubbing
foreheads with
Nakire as a sign of
friendship

The War Dance

Chief Baou of the Tigre clan

Papa, please, please . . .
please let me keep it!

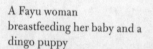

A Fayu woman
breastfeeding her baby and a
dingo puppy

Papa's office (on the left) and our 'guesthouse' (on the right)

Papa with a night-time visitor

Sitting with Faisa and Klausu-Bosa on the steps of our house in Foida

War!

Me (far right) with
Tuare (middle) and Christian
practising our shooting skills

With Christian, being held by a
Sefoidi warrior

The three of us after a successful
day on the jungle slide

Nakire and his wife Fusai

Nakire with a dead crocodile
after a successful hunt

Our new house with a beautiful
jungle view

Trekking through the swamps to
reach our new house on the hill

Among the Fayu
women

Mama with her new
school

Klaus-Peter and Doris Kuegler in
Foida, 2000

Papa with
Chief Kologwoi (right)
and Kloru (left),
Tuare's father

now had the right to kill Isori out of revenge. Chief Baou was afraid for his son, all ready imagining him as dead.

Our family sat around the kitchen table trying to decide how to handle it. Finally Mama said, 'Klaus, you know in the Bible it says that when someone takes something from you unjustly, repay them with kindness and give them something extra in addition. Why don't you just take him this nice piece of crocodile meat and tell him that we're not angry.'

We all nodded in appreciation of this idea. A Fayu came and told us that Isori was hiding in the jungle, panicked and terrified about what Papa or his own father would do to him.

Papa took the meat and went to find him. I followed along behind. We wandered up the small path that led to Chief Baou's hut. The whole family was sitting there; our arrival increased their agitation. Papa asked Chief Baou where his son was, explaining that he wanted to talk to him. I looked at the chief's face; never had I seen this powerful man look so forlorn.

Chief Baou called for his son, who eventually stepped out of the brush, shaking with fear. Papa slowly approached Isori and did the unthinkable. He took the boy in his arms and told Isori that he wasn't angry and to prove it had brought him this nice piece of meat as a gift. Isori took the meat with great confusion and promptly disappeared back into the jungle.

In this moment, Chief Baou looked at Papa with tears in his eyes. Nobody said a word. Here was a man known for his brutality. He had never given or received mercy or forgiveness. What the white man did was completely unimaginable to him. It was this gesture that paved the way for Chief Baou to become a peacemaker.

As we were returning to our house, I had an insight into my father's heart and saw more clearly the thing that guided his work with the Fayu. He always taught us that love is stronger than hate, that this is a truth that cannot be taught by words alone but must be lived. Our example would change the hearts of these people. As I walked behind him, it became clear that I had just witnessed something special. It was only a small gesture, but for these forgotten people with a tradition of hate, it was a step along a new path – the path to peace.

There were many false steps along this journey. Forgiveness and peace cannot be learned in a single day. Yet today, the Fayu do live in peace, except, of course, for some conflict that is common to all humankind. They have learned to resolve conflicts peacefully, seeking cooperative solutions rather than vengeance. It wasn't always easy. Some days, all of us became discouraged and despairing. But no one gave up. They became a people united by a common goal, and they strove together to reach it.

The meat incident was not the only time the Fayu stole from us. Every time we returned from Danau Bira, a good portion of our household would be missing. This was a difficult situation for Mama and Papa. Finding replacements in the jungle was expensive at best and often simply impossible. They kept hoping that the Fayu would change. But that hope was dashed with every return to Foida; change had not yet come. My parents waited patiently anyway.

The stealing occasionally had its bright sides. We found it rather amusing when a chief ran around wearing Mama's granny panties or wore her slip as a hat. They also loved to steal the nails from Papa's toolbox. Since the Fayu didn't use hammers, he always wondered what they did with them. And then one day, Papa saw them wearing the nails as nose jewelry.

Not long after the incident with Isori, Papa was returning from Kordesi, where he had received a shipment of supplies. Among them was a new, blue plastic bucket for Mama. Ours had broken, and Mama was eagerly awaiting this one.

A young Fayu man went over to the boat and began to nag Papa for a knife. Papa told him that he didn't have one and that he would have to wait for the next supply trip. This went on for several minutes before the young man turned away in anger. As he stalked off, he picked up a rock, turned, and suddenly hurled it full strength at Papa. It barely missed him (thank God!) and hit the new bucket instead, cracking it wide open. Thinking of Mama's need for it as well as the great effort he'd made in order to get it, Papa lost his temper. He began to run in fury at the offender, and the chase was on.

Still in full stride, Papa noticed that all of the Fayu were watching him intently. Perhaps they were thinking, *Well look at Klausu. We have never seen him so angry. He'll explode at any moment.* Just as he reached the young man, Papa had a sudden change of heart. His anger just disappeared and was replaced with peace. Papa later told me that it was a present from heaven. In this moment, he understood the true cost of forgiveness.

When he caught the boy, Papa reached out and hugged him, and then they rubbed foreheads together in the Fayu gesture of friendship. The other Fayu watched in surprise, again confronted by the foreign concept of forgiveness.

I was standing next to Christian during all this excitement and couldn't help but think of poor, bucketless Mama.

'It's lucky for you that you didn't break the bucket. You'd have gotten into a lot more trouble than the Fayu did,' Christian commented. I nodded in relief that for once I wasn't the culprit.

It is difficult to describe the importance of a bucket in the jungle, especially to someone who lives in a world where everything is easily replaceable. In the West, a bucket is just a bucket. But imagine that you live in the jungle, and the drums of rainwater have run dry. You need water to wash yourself and to flush the toilet, to do laundry, and to clean sweet potatoes in the river. Now imagine doing all this without a bucket or any large container, and you'll begin to see how important that bucket was to us. And now it was broken before we could even use it. Mama would once again have to improvise solutions for the daily chores.

It must not have been easy for my mother, who had grown up in Germany and wasn't used to this sort of life. I admire her and have great respect for the competence with which she kept our lives running in the midst of such difficult circumstances. Mama never became angry or frustrated when something didn't work. She simply tried to find a way around it. The constant stealing must have been so hard during those years. It is quite something that she never became bitter.

As one of many attempts to prevent stealing, Papa once tried building a fake wall in order to create a secret space in our house. We gathered everything we weren't taking with us to Danau Bira, put it in drums, and hid it behind the wall.

But when we came back, the wall had been broken, and everything was gone. All of the bedsheets, clothing, cutlery, dishes, towels, soap – simply everything. Mama and Papa were discouraged and didn't know what to do. We all sat around the table, looking at each other in silence.

Suddenly, there was a quiet knocking on the door. Papa opened it to see Nakire standing there, saying, 'Hey Klausu, follow me.' We all followed him outside and saw several

Iyarike men standing there. They told us to wait and then disappeared into the jungle. As we stood there, we heard rustling in the brush. To our great surprise, we saw Nakire and the men rolling our drums out of the undergrowth. Nakire proudly explained that he had beaten the thieves to our house and hidden the drums in the jungle. We were thrilled! This was the first time we saw the Fayu act in a way that was outside of what their culture dictated. For us, it was a small miracle.

Over time, the thieving slowly decreased. One day, it stopped completely. We had recently returned from Danau Bira when we heard a chorus of voices outside our house. We went outside to see what was going on and saw them all standing there. The men of all four Fayu clans: Iyarike, Sefoidi, Tigre and Tearue.

They were lined up along the riverbank and came to us one by one. To our utter amazement, they laid at Papa's feet everything they had ever stolen. Pots, clothing, knives, spoons, boxes, fishhooks, rusty nails and so on. And at the head of the line was Chief Baou.

Most of the items were in such bad condition that we could barely recognize them, let alone use them. But we were still overjoyed. This was a special moment for us. Led by Chief Baou, the Fayu made a collective decision not to steal from us any more.

27

JUDITH GROWS UP

Our family wasn't always together. One time, the helicopter came to pick up Mama, who had to make a shopping trip to Jayapura because the rice bag was empty, the tea and coffee almost gone, and the canned vegetables running low. So Mama left, promising to bring us back a present. We happily waved good-bye and dreamed of what she might get us.

Shortly after her departure, I woke up in the middle of the night to a quiet noise. It was pitch black outside; there was only a weak light coming from the bathroom. Judith wasn't in her bed, and I could see her kneeling on the bathroom floor through the gap in the curtains. I knew something was wrong, as Judith never got up during the night, especially not in order to sit on the bathroom floor.

I got out from under my mosquito net and crept over to the curtain. 'Judith,' I whispered, 'is everything okay?' All I heard was a muffled sob. Now really worried, I slipped into the bathroom and was shocked at my sister's appearance. In the light of two candles, I saw her nightgown laying on the floor, spotted with blood. Large tears rolled down her cheeks as she wiped the floor with a hand towel.

My first thought was *snakebite*! But then I figured that it must have come from a larger animal, since there was too much blood for a snakebite. 'Are you going to die now, Judith?' I asked, wide-eyed. Judith just shook her head.

'Did you cut yourself? Should I go get Papa?'

'No!' she exclaimed a little too loudly. We both jumped at the sound of her voice. I sat down next to her, staring at the blood, and thought it over. Then I had it. Judith had cancer! Mama had recently told us about this disease after a friend of hers died from it. I had bugged Judith so much recently that she must have caught cancer herself. Now she would probably die, and it was all my fault.

I started to cry. 'It's my fault,' I sobbed. 'I'm always so mean to you. Just last week I put worms under your pillow, and now you've become so upset that you've got cancer. I'm sure to go to hell.' To my surprise, Judith started giggling. Had she completely lost it? Maybe the cancer had all ready reached her brain.

'Sabine,' she giggled, 'I don't have cancer. I've got my period.'

'What is that?' I asked. With that much blood involved, it had to be something serious.

'Don't you ever pay attention when Mama explains something?' Judith asked in frustration. 'When a girl gets older and her body is ready to have children, she bleeds every month for a couple of days.'

'Are you going to have a baby soon?' I asked excitedly.

'I hope not!' my sister whispered in horror.

'Well, Christian and I will build you a hut in the jungle

tomorrow like the Fayu men do for their women.' Since Judith didn't have a man, I decided that Christian and I would have to take care of her.

'But I don't want to go alone into the jungle!' Judith said. 'You have to!'

'Mama doesn't go into the jungle every month, so I don't think I have to.'

I had to think about that for a bit. Why didn't Mama go into the jungle every month? I badly wanted to build a hut, and this was my opportunity. Mama wasn't there, and Papa could be easily convinced to go along with most things. After all, this concerned my sister's health!

But then another thought occurred to me. 'Judith, why don't you have a man?'

'Because I am too young,' was her answer.

'But Mama says that the Fayu girls get stolen at nine or ten years old. Why hasn't anybody stolen you?'

'Because I'm not a Fayu girl, and in Germany, people don't get married until they're much older. Mama was twenty-eight when she married Papa.'

'That old?!' I asked, horrified.

Judith grinned. 'Besides, I don't want to get married. Always having to work, preparing sago, watching the kids. Besides, I don't want to get big breasts.'

I had to agree with her there. That didn't sound very appealing. 'I won't get married either,' I decided. 'I'll live on a farm and have lots of animals.'

Judith just sighed. 'Can you help me clean up?' she finally asked. I nodded, and together we finished cleaning the floor and put fresh sheets on her bed.

'Goodnight,' I whispered through my mosquito net.

'Thank you,' Judith whispered back.

The next morning, Judith refused to get out of bed.

When Papa called her for the third time to come to breakfast, I couldn't keep the news to myself any more.

'Judith got her period,' I whispered to him.

He looked at me with big eyes as I enthusiastically nodded my head. 'Now Christian and I have to build her a hut in the jungle.'

'Is she dying?' Christian asked anxiously.

'No,' Papa sighed. 'She won't die, and hopefully I'll live as well.'

After breakfast, he went to the radio. 'Foida, here. Foida, here. We have an emergency. I must get a message to Jayapura.'

'Foida, this is Jayapura. What's the situation?' came the worried voice over the radio.

'Jim,' Papa replied, 'I have to speak to my wife. Can you please give her the message that Judith has got her period and I don't know what to do.'

A scream of protest came echoing out of the bedroom. 'Do you have to tell all of Irian Jaya that I got my period!' Judith shrieked angrily. 'It's nobody's business! And if I want to stay in bed all week, I will!'

I rolled my eyes. Why did Judith always have to be so dramatic! Poor Papa stood helplessly by the radio.

'Maybe we could build you a hut in the jungle,' Christian offered helpfully.

'No!' Judith shrieked back, her voice reaching the upper registers.

To all of our relief, Mama came back two days later. She took over and life calmed back down.

28

MY FRIEND FAISA

When we first came to the Fayu, only the boys would play with us. The Fayu girls were very shy and wouldn't participate in the wild games we so loved. I don't remember a single time when they ever played 'crocodile' in the river or hunted insects with bows and arrows. The reason for this is the clearly defined gender roles in their culture.

But there was one Fayu girl around my age who liked to hang around and watch me. I don't remember how our friendship began or who spoke first, but at some point I realized that she had become part of my life. Her name was Faisa.

Faisa was an exceptionally pretty girl. She had big, clear eyes and flawless skin unmarked by fungal growth or other diseases. When she smiled, her face lit up the jungle. As we spent more and more time together, Faisa began teaching me how to do the jobs of Fayu women. For example, how to craft long threads from tree bark and then weave fishing traps out of them. Or how to properly roll a small animal in sago and cook it. Other times, like after swimming, Faisa would sit next to me on a log, and we would warm ourselves in the sun. And sometimes we just sat around the fire.

When we were about ten years old, Faisa hit puberty, and her breasts began to develop. I knew that Fayu girls at this stage of development could be taken as wives, but I simply couldn't imagine that happening to Faisa. She was my friend, the same age as me. From my point of view, Faisa was still as much of a child as I was.

Faisa also had a 'best girl friend' from among the Fayu girls – a girl whose name I can no longer remember. She was older than us, and I didn't really like her. She got on our nerves sometimes and would laugh shrilly and loudly when we did something funny. Her skin was covered with ringworm, and she was missing some teeth. She could also be really mean when she didn't like something. But I played with her anyway. With so few playmates, one can't be picky. And one day, she proved herself to be a true and brave friend.

It was late one afternoon, and I was playing with Faisa on the sandbank. We were completely engrossed in the game when I heard shouting. It was Faisa's friend, but this wasn't her usual yelling; there was something different in her tone. I heard the warning in her voice but saw nothing threatening. No boar, no snake, no enemy warriors. Then Faisa's friend came sprinting out of the jungle, jumped into one of the canoes tied at the tip of the sandbank, and madly paddled toward us. Was she in danger herself, or was she trying to warn us about something?

Faisa looked around in confusion but couldn't figure out what the problem was. As she neared us, her friend gesticulated wildly in the direction of the village. We turned around and saw Nakire's brother running toward us with a machete in hand.

Faisa panicked, began screaming, and ran to the river's edge. I started to panic too when I realized what was going on. This aggressive man wanted to marry Faisa, and she must have refused. Faisa ran as fast as she could toward the oncoming canoe while I kept shouting, 'Hau! Hau! Hau! (No! No! No!)'

Nakire's brother could run very fast and was rapidly overtaking Faisa. More and more Fayu gathered on the riverbanks in response to the commotion, silently watching the scene unfold. Why was nobody helping us? Why were they all standing around with expressionless faces? I didn't know what to do, how to help. But it was obvious to me that when he caught Faisa, the man would beat her until she agreed to marry him. And then there would be no going back.

Nakire's brother was only a few yards behind Faisa when she suddenly stumbled. My breathing stopped. He reached her and swung the machete. But she was quicker, managing to turn to one side so that she avoided the blade. Faisa jumped up and ran into the water, where her friend was only a few yards away. Nakire's brother tried to grab her, but Faisa reached the canoe just ahead of him.

She pulled herself into the boat as her friend paddled into deeper and faster currents. Nakire's brother stood in the water, swinging the machete in rage. I can still see Faisa's desperate expression as the current carried her into the unknown.

I watched them until they disappeared around the curve and was deeply saddened. Day after day, I awaited her return, but for nothing. She never came back. Faisa couldn't return because it was unlikely she would succeed in escaping the next time.

Life seemed empty without Faisa. I missed her smile, her camaraderie, and her joy in teaching me new skills. Years later I learned that Faisa was forced to go into hiding for a long time in the jungle. She eventually met a man whom she liked in return and agreed to marry him.

Now I had witnessed firsthand what could happen when a Fayu girl rejected a man. It shook me deeply. In general, Fayu women had little say about whom they married. Today this has changed, but perhaps now it is clearer to you what a remarkable choice Nakire made. His relationship with Fusai was a shining exception in the darkness of their out-dated system of marriage.

In the West, we are used to extensive dating rituals: meaningful glances, intimacy developed over the course of time spent together, the exchange of rings. But the Fayu culture had none of that – not even a wedding ceremony. Sometimes the father of the girl decided whom she would marry. In that case, he gave her over to the man, who simply took her home with him.

If a man wanted to marry a certain woman but her father disagreed, the man would just kidnap her. The father would have often set guards around his daughter, so the man had to wait until an unprotected moment. Then he would grab her and force her to go with him. In some cases, her protector might be killed. Either way, he would keep her in hiding until she agreed to marry him, often with the coercion of violence.

What I found interesting about this custom was that the woman's family would not contest the marriage when the couple finally returned from hiding. Even the previously resistant father would condone the union. The subject would not be brought up again, and life would go on as usual – the woman now living with her new husband. How most women felt about it, I cannot venture to say, except in the case of Faisa, who made her feelings abundantly clear.

29

JUNGLE TIME

The night before my eleventh birthday, I could barely sleep as my anticipation mounted. Mama and Judith got up early that morning, and the smell of coffee filled our small house. I jumped out of bed, but Mama sent me back; the preparations hadn't been completed yet. Christian crawled under the blanket with me, and together we waited for the big moment. We celebrated our birthdays together since they are only two days apart – his on 23 December and mine on Christmas Day.

Finally, it was time. Judith opened the curtain that separated the bedroom from the living area, and we raced past her to the dining table. There was a beautifully arranged table before our eyes, complete with colourful napkins, candles and most important, presents. Papa was all ready sitting at the table, and Mama was busy making our favourite breakfast – pancakes covered in cinnamon and sugar. They smelled wonderful. Our eyes lit up as we inspected the colourful, shiny paper that wrapped our gifts. We were too excited to eat and so were allowed to open our presents first.

It is still a mystery to me how Mama and Papa always managed to hide our gifts so long. As children, we simply accepted it as parental magic. Though we were hundreds of jungle-filled miles away from the nearest store, the wonderful presents would just suddenly appear.

I don't remember everything I got that day, but one present stands out in my memory. It was my first watch – and what a watch it was! It had a black wristband and hands that glowed in the dark. And best of all, it was waterproof. It was the best present ever.

I strapped the watch around my thin, brown wrist, feeling modern and grown up. Now I could tell everybody what time it was. Unlike in the West, however, no one really wanted to know. In the rainforest, you don't need a watch to tell the time. Wearing it simply makes you look cool.

During my years in West Papua, I developed a different sense of time. Time moves much more slowly there than elsewhere – creeping from sunup to sundown. It is consistent in its snail's pace over the days, weeks and years.

And I began to adjust to the slowness of time. Nobody was in a hurry. No one worried about being late for an appointment. What big event is going to happen anyway in a place where each day looks like the one before it? If you had agreed to meet someone, you simply waited until the person showed up. If the person didn't come today, he or she might come tomorrow. If the person never came, it was either because he or she lost the desire to meet you or because death had found the person along the way.

Even my physical movements slowed down, as the extreme heat made speed difficult. If you moved too energetically, you would quickly tire and become weak. And

why be tired and weak? After all, there was always tomorrow or the day after that stretching out into an eternity
before you. I had the feeling that my life was standing still,
and in comparison to my life today, it was.

Adding further to this effect was the lack of real sea-
sons – it was always summer. So the days, weeks and months
flowed together in such a long, unbroken highway that I
couldn't tell you whether it was June or November. The
only month I paid attention to was December, my birthday
month.

On the other hand, there was a daily type of time meas-
urement that was very precise, and the entire jungle –
animal, plant and human – was subject to it. Because of
that, the sun, moon and insect activity were better time
indicators for me than the metal around my arm. There is
a plant that closes its leaves at noon to protect itself from the
heat and opens again at 5 pm. And then came the mosquitoes. At exactly 6 pm, dark clouds of hungry bloodsuckers
would come streaming out of their hiding places.

The clock of the jungle was precise, didn't have to be
wound, and never had to be adjusted. At exactly 6 am every
day, the sun came up. When it was directly overhead, it was
time to look for shade and get something to eat. And coin-
cidentally, my watch agreed! It read 12:00. The presence of
the moon called us to bed, and the next morning, the cycle
would begin again.

When I moved to Europe, it took a long time to get used
to the speed with which life flows. A day in the West is like
a week in the jungle, and a week is like a month. Sometimes
a sense of panic would set in as I felt time slipping out of my
grasp. I had the feeling that everything was out of control,
moving faster than I could keep up with.

In the jungle, though, the days flowed over me. I took life

as it came. There was no need to get upset when plans changed, which was a common occurrence. Our plans were as relaxed as time itself. We learned never to plan more than a week ahead, as one never knew what would happen in the meantime. Sometimes the boat motor would break, other times the aeroplane. There might be a flood, or the pilot might be in bed with malaria. We got used to the fact that our plans might change from one day to the next. And we learned not to let this be a source of stress.

The western concept of planning ten years or more in advance was very strange to me. It was a new way of thinking that took years to understand and accept. I saw evidence everywhere around me that planning was important but didn't know how to do it for myself. Sure, there are a plethora of books and courses about time management, but none of them was geared for a person like me, who had such a profoundly different understanding of time itself. It wasn't until about two years ago – when I turned thirty – that I learned to make plans for my future. It took me over a decade to understand and be able to adopt the western approach to time.

30

GOOD SPIRIT, BAD SPIRIT

I didn't often speak with my Fayu friends about our feelings or beliefs. We were too preoccupied with everyday things – our games, food, people and animals. But situations occasionally arose that led to deeper conversations.

I was once standing on a sandbank with Bebe when a horrible stench filled the air. Several canoes had just arrived from upriver, and in one of them was a dead boy, maybe twelve or thirteen years old. His body was distended and covered with flies. When I saw it, I felt sick to my stomach.

The boy's mother sat in the boat and smiled at me as though she was proud to have brought us her dead boy. Usually, Fayu leave their dead in their huts. The woman began to lift the corpse out of the canoe when Nakire came running up and told her not to bring the body on shore. She became furious and started screaming that someone had killed her son with a curse. The screaming repeated over and over, but Nakire remained steadfast. The woman finally left in her canoe, cursing loudly as she went.

'Surely Tohre killed that boy,' said Bebe nervously, as the mourning mother disappeared from view. 'Tonight, I'll stay in my hut. He might come back and kill me too.'

'Who is Tohre?' I asked.

Bebe carefully looked around, moved close to me, and whispered, 'He is the evil spirit. He comes out of the jungle at night to eat people.'

'If he eats people, why is the boy's body still there?'

'He doesn't eat the body. Much worse – he eats the life in the body.'

'So what is the name of the good spirit?' I wanted to know.

Bebe was confused. 'What good spirit? There is no good spirit.'

'There must be a good spirit if there is an evil spirit,' I said, just as confused.

Bebe gave me a blank look. He seemed quite sure that there was no good spirit. *How sad,* I thought to myself. *No wonder they live in such fear.*

That night I had a nightmare. A figure stood in the doorway, large and ugly, with blackened skin and sharp teeth. It approached my bed, watching me. I crawled underneath the blankets, hoping that it couldn't pierce the mosquito net. But maybe it could. Would my life be eaten now? I was so afraid that I didn't even dare to scream, so I closed my eyes and prayed.

When I woke up the next morning, I consoled myself with the thought that it had only been a bad dream. But what if there really was an evil spirit that ate the life inside you?

Life in this primeval forest is full of mystical stories and experiences. The jungle is a world in which fantasy and reality seem to mix. But I had always believed that there is a good spirit, one that loved and protected us and was stronger than its evil opponent.

I explained this to Bebe the next time I saw him. I told him that he shouldn't be afraid, because we believed in Good. And it is only this belief that gave us the courage to give up everything and move to a strange new world. It was our belief in Good that caused us to never give up, even if times were difficult. In the end, Good would triumph over Evil.

Bebe sat down next to me, took my hand, and chewed on my fingers. This was a Fayu sign of close friendship. Together we gazed into the fire and listened to the songs of the night. Yes, we believed in the Good Spirit. Here in the lost valley, we were close to Him. We could sense Him and felt safe in His presence.

31

THE DECIDING WAR

A dramatic event occurred along the long, slow path to peace. It marked a turning point for the Fayu. Once again, two clans met in front of our house. They began to argue, and soon the war dance commenced, giving all appearances that it would last until sundown.

Mama managed to defuse the last several confrontations by playing music at maximum volume on a cassette player. To our surprise, the music managed to pierce the loud chanting of the Fayu. One by one the enraged warriors came and sat in front of the house to listen to the strange music, and peace prevailed.

But this time, the music didn't help. *Ooh-wa, ooh-wa, ooh-wa.* It went on for hours as Christian and I watched from the window. I could tell by their movements and the pitch of their yelling that the warriors had reached the trance state. The Tigre and the Iyarike were airing their old grievances: cycle after cycle of death, blame, vengeance, more death and so on, until eventually no one knew where it had started. Revenge had become its own goal.

Judith was sitting on her bed, scared, while Mama tried to calm her by reading her a story. Hour upon hour of the war chant frayed Judith's nerves. This, coupled with the knowledge that at any moment people could start killing each other, began to create an unbearable intensity. Although we had only witnessed one war that resulted in bloodshed, the memory of it lay heavily on Judith's heart. Finally, it became too much for her. Judith held her hands over her ears and started screaming. And then she couldn't stop.

Everything started to move quickly then. Papa's anger hit the boiling point, and he did something that he admits today could have cost him his life. Papa grabbed a machete, threw open the door, and ran out into the middle of the melee. Christian and I held our breath. We had never seen our father like this.

The tension in the air was reaching a breaking point. The warriors had notched their arrows and were pointing them at one another. Their bodies dripped with sweat, and their eyes were glazed over. This is the condition that greeted Papa when he ran out into the middle of them.

When Papa had positioned himself between the two groups, he swung out with his machete and cut through the bowstring of the nearest warrior. The Fayu just stared through him. So Papa grabbed the bow of the next warrior and cut its string. Then another, and another. Suddenly silence descended as everyone stared at Papa with disbelief. He grabbed the two war chiefs and dragged them to our house. Judith's screams still echoed from the house, as she was beyond any solace.

'Do you hear that? Do you hear the screams of my daughter?' Papa roared. 'She's screaming because she's terrified. Listen to what you're doing to my family.'

Nobody said a word. I stared in amazement at the scene before me.

'I can't do this to my family any more,' Papa continued. Then he turned to the chieftains and said, 'I'll give you two options. Either you stop warring around this house and go somewhere else to fight, or I will take my family and leave. Make your decision.'

With these words, he spun on his heels and came back into the house, slamming the door behind him. Papa sat down on the bench, his entire body shaking. We didn't dare move or speak but just looked back and forth between Papa and the Fayu warriors outside, who were talking among themselves.

Judith's screams had faded to whimpers, and she said that she wanted to leave this place. Papa went to her and asked if he should request a helicopter to take her back to Danau Bira. She said yes, so with a heavy heart, he went to the radio and organized a flight for the next day.

Shortly afterward, we heard a quiet knocking on our door. Chief Baou stood there and asked Papa to come outside. Papa followed him and stood in front of the assembled warriors.

Chief Baou said that he was speaking for everyone present and that none of them wanted Papa or his family to leave. He went on to say that we had brought them hope and they loved us. They were sorry that their behaviour had scared his daughter so much. 'Please, Klausu, stay with us. We won't war around your house any more. We want our hearts to be good. Please stay here with your family. We will protect them and promise that nothing will ever happen to them. Please, Klausu.'

Papa was struck dumb by relief and astonishment. He looked around at the warriors who had, only moments before, been ready to kill each other. They now stood united in front of him, asking him to stay.

We stayed. Judith did leave the next day and was taken to Danau Bira, where she lived for a short time with the pilot and his family. The Fayu sang songs of mourning when the helicopter lifted off with her. This was perhaps the first time they understood the effect of their actions on us.

That evening, Chief Kologwoi picked up a large piece of raw meat and commanded his warriors to line up in a row. The first in line took his bow and pulled back the bowstring as far as he could. Then one after another, all the Iyarike warriors stepped through the drawn bow. Chief Kologwoi went last and then walked over to Chief Baou. Bowing slightly, he handed him the piece of meat. I saw Papa's eyes light up. He hurriedly called for Nakire and asked him what had just happened.

Nakire replied that someone from Chief Kologwoi's clan had killed a Tigre warrior, one of Chief Baou's men. The Tigre now had the right to avenge themselves on the Iyarike. This was the precipitating cause of the recent war. But the two chiefs had settled on another solution. The ceremony of the drawn-back bow and the gift of meat indicated reconciliation. The chiefs would now cook and eat the meat together. Nakire commented that 'once the fires of revenge have been quenched, the way is open for reconciliation'.

On this day the Iyarike and the Tigre were the first of the clans to make peace with one another. That peace has lasted to this day. When Judith returned to Foida, they threw a big celebration of peace and joy.

That was the last time we had war around our house. After that, Chief Baou instituted a new rule: everyone who came to visit us had to leave their bow and arrow in their hut or canoe. And so the area around our house became a war-free zone where members of all clans could assemble without fear. Soon, each of the clans had members living near us.

Slowly, the mood in the jungle changed. There was now a calm that even I could feel. A new era had begun for this small nation. This was the first time in living memory that the four clans had ever lived in such close proximity. And they did so without fear. Clan relations slowly improved. Children laughed, fathers held peaceful discussions and mothers prepared sago together. The constant anxiety faded from Tuare's eyes.

There were still occasional disagreements, after which the wounded came to our house for treatment. But these became increasingly rare. Whenever we were in Foida, the Fayu would come out of their different regions and live together with us in the village. When we were gone for a while, they would return into the jungle. They are hunter-gatherers and will always remain so – true people of the jungle. But they had finally found the peace with one another that they so desired.

32

TIME PASSES

Tuare looked at me one day and said that it wouldn't be long before someone would steal me for marriage. Astonished, I asked him why. 'That,' he said, pointing at the small breasts developing underneath my shirt. 'You're becoming a woman.' I looked down and was a little surprised myself. Tuare asked if I would now leave the Fayu in order to go find a man.

'No,' I replied, laughing. 'I won't get married yet. Maybe in many, many moons.' I had just turned twelve.

Tuare seemed worried with this response. 'If you wait that long, you'll be too old and no man will want to steal you.'

'That doesn't matter, Tuare. Then I just won't get married and will stay here for ever.'

'Asahaego (agreed),' Tuare said with a satisfied nod of his head. And so the subject of growing up was settled.

I lived in a sheltered world. In my mind, the universe consisted of the jungle and the Fayu, and I couldn't imagine anything else. Over the years I had been thoroughly transformed into a jungle girl, body and soul. But as much as I would have liked to live for ever in this childhood, time kept advancing.

My life changed one night by the light of the kerosene lamps. Papa told us that we would soon be returning to Germany for a home furlough. I was suddenly more excited than I thought possible. I couldn't begin to imagine this world about which I had heard so much. Stores, cars, tall buildings, running warm water and toys. *It must be like heaven,* I thought.

I imagined all the new things I would buy and the many white people who would greet me and invite me to their houses. The thoughts were almost too much for me and made it hard to fall asleep. The next morning I delightedly informed Tuare about our plans. He didn't seem quite as enthusiastic. Looking rather unhappy, he kept asking when we were coming back and why we were leaving in the first place. I couldn't answer the last part but told him that we wouldn't be gone for too long.

A few weeks later, it was time. We packed everything into our boat and said our good-byes. Tuare came to me with tears in his eyes and was distraught from head to toe. He stood in front of me and pressed something into my hand. It was a crocodile tooth. It brought tears to my eyes – not because of the tooth but because of what was in it.

There are three stages of friendship in the Fayu culture. The first is marked by napping next to one another, with forefingers entwined. The second involves gently chewing on the other person's fingers. And the third and highest stage is expressed by exchanging crocodile teeth. Each person places a few strands of his or her hair inside of the hollow tooth and then ties it around the other person's neck.

The Fayu believe that in order to curse a person, you must have a piece of his or her hair. So by giving someone your hair, you are indicating that you trust him or her not to use it to hurt you. With this gesture, you entrust this friend with your life. And this is what Tuare had just done. Leaving behind such a dear friend filled me with great sorrow.

The currents carried us downriver as the Fayu sang their mourning song. The sound of their sorrow followed us for miles. A short time later, we left Indonesia and returned to our parents' home.

33

VACATION TO THE HOMELAND

I recently called my sister, who lives with her husband and son in America. 'Judith, do you remember our furlough?' I asked.

A moment of silence. 'Weird. Not really,' she answered.

This actually is rather strange, because I don't either. I only remember fragments. We had planned on staying for only a year in Germany but ended up staying longer. During our furlough, my parents started working for a different organization, called YPPM, and it took a long time to get new work visas.

The first few months in Germany were exciting. For the first time, we saw things that we had only read or heard about: stores, the Autobahn, central heating and especially snow.

The highlight of our time in Germany was a visit to my grandmother (Oma in German) in Bad Segeberg. Oma had sent us wonderful letters and packages over the years, and she remains dear to my heart.

The icy-cold wind blew as dark clouds circled overhead.

I had once again forgotten to wear tights and was securely wrapped in a blanket. Suddenly, I heard Christian shout excitedly, 'Look out the window!'

And then I saw. Huge snowflakes coming down from the sky. The three of us ran to the window and looked out in wonder. We barely dared to breathe as the snow fell without making a sound. *Please don't let it stop*, I prayed up to heaven, and my prayer was answered. It began snowing more heavily, and soon everything was covered by a layer of white.

'Germans must be really thankful to experience something this beautiful every year,' Judith sighed.

Oma was amused at our fascination with the snow. 'Well Judith, if you like it so much, why don't you go ahead and get started with the shovelling,' she said drily.

'Can we go outside?' I asked excitedly, and ran out without waiting for an answer. Snowflakes danced through the air, and I stuck out my tongue to catch them.

'Don't eat them,' Christian called out worriedly. 'They might be poisonous.' This was a hard-and-fast jungle rule: don't eat unknown substances, since you never knew which ones might kill you.

Quickly, I spat out the contents of my mouth and cleaned my tongue on my shirt. But a grinning Judith calmed us down, saying, 'It's only frozen water – like ice cream.' Christian and I looked at Judith skeptically, but when even she began to catch snowflakes on her tongue, we believed her and joined in.

I noticed an odd pain in my feet and suddenly realized that I was barefoot in the snow. With a mighty shriek I ran back into the warm house. 'And there she is again,' Mama said. 'Well Sabine, did you have fun?' Ignoring her, I threw on some shoes, grabbed a jacket and ran back outside. We spent the rest of the afternoon playing together in the snow.

My parents knew to expose us to the culture slowly, so we were quite sheltered and had no TV or radio. But there were still many things that we had difficulty understanding and adapting to. For example, the first time we went into a grocery store, our jaws dropped. Christian broke down in tears of confusion at the choices. Judith couldn't be dragged away from the chocolate aisle. Which variety should she buy? She had never seen so much chocolate in her whole life and kept running back to the aisle to double-check her choice until Mama finally decided to buy her one of each kind.

I found the people in the store as interesting as the food. It was a shock to see that many white people all in one place. And so many of them were fat! In the jungle, if someone has a big stomach, it is the result of intestinal worms.

'Does everyone here have worms?' I asked worriedly. Mama laughed and explained that here it was the result of eating too much. That was rather interesting, and I wondered if I could get a big stomach if I ate a lot. Sadly, I stayed rail thin, since we couldn't tolerate the rich German food very well. At home, Mama usually cooked the same kind of food that we ate in Foida, but at Oma's, there was always chocolate and cake.

'I don't feel so good,' I whined, having yet again eaten three pieces of cake at one sitting.

'That's your own fault,' Mama answered with a remarkable lack of sympathy.

The concept of a never-ending supply of food was incomprehensible to us. One time, after I had eaten the last piece of chocolate, Christian cried bitterly. So Mama took him to the store and bought him more. By the time they returned home, Christian had eaten the entire thing 'so that Sabine can't take it away from me'.

'But Christian, we can always go to the store and get another one,' Mama informed him.

'Yes, but what happens when the store runs out?'

'Then they'll order more from the factory.'

'But what if the factory runs out?' Christian wanted to know.

'Factories don't run out of chocolate. And even if one did, you could just go to another factory.' Mama got the feeling that teaching us to be German would be a long and difficult road.

Christian got upset at the impossibility of this claim. He stamped his foot and cried out, 'But if every German ate chocolate every day, then eventually even the factories would run out.'

Full of frustration, Mama considered how she could give a satisfactory answer. Then she had an idea. 'Christian,' she said, 'you're right. If, for example, there's a war, then the chocolate would run out.'

'I knew it!' he said with great satisfaction. War is something he understood, and that explanation solved the problem for him.

Nothing about our life in the jungle prepared us for the great abundance of things in the West. We were used to twice-a-year shopping trips and having the problems of having little storage space and difficulty transporting supplies. So even Mama had difficulty resisting the urge to shop in large quantities.

As time passed and our return to Indonesia was delayed, I was placed in a school in Bad Segeberg. That was the scariest event of my life, so I was quite relieved when my parents pulled me out after a few weeks. The principal had told my parents that I was too old to transfer into a German school system.

Shortly after that, we left Germany and flew to the United States. *Another new culture with weird people behaving oddly,* I thought to myself. I felt an increasing longing to return to the jungle and began daydreaming a lot. My body was in the West, but my thoughts were far away. It was a time I'd rather not remember. I cried a lot at night, and my siblings didn't have an easy time either. The situation got worse and worse for us kids, which only served to increase my parents' worry. We felt like outsiders in western culture in both Germany and America and simply wanted to return to the jungle.

I hit puberty and gained a lot of weight. I ate out of frustration and homesickness. It did help a bit hearing Papa give speeches and show films about the Fayu during our time in the West.

Occasionally people would come up to him after a presentation and say, 'People don't live that way any more. You made it up for television, right?' In the beginning, I was offended by those comments but learned to laugh about them. I imagined telling the Fayu about the Western world and realized that they wouldn't believe me either.

Then, after what seemed like for ever, it came time to return. The day we received our visas was one of pure joy. Papa immediately bought tickets, and a short time later, we left for Indonesia. When I saw the jungle underneath me, I cried with joy. I could barely believe it. I had come home again. The time I had spent in 'civilization' had left a big mark on me, but I didn't know that at the time.

The reunion with the Fayu was incredibly emotional. We hugged and danced around like small children. The Fayu cried and told us that they had given up hope of ever seeing us again. That evening, I sat around the fire with my old gang: Christian, Tuare, Dihida, Ohri, Bebe, Isori, Diro,

Klausu Bosa and the rest. We had all grown up a bit, and yet our relationships remained the same. We were a family, and as Christian said while preparing for bed that night, we would always stay that way. As I climbed under my mosquito net, I felt happy for the first time in a long time.

Yes, I thought to myself, *this is where I belong.* And with this thought, I fell asleep.

34

THE JUNGLE CALLS

Full of energy and exhilaration, we resumed our previous life as though we'd only been gone a few days. But even with the best intentions, certain changes could not be denied. Our house was literally falling apart. Papa had all ready fallen through the floor twice, as the termite-infested floorboards cracked underneath his weight. Additionally, the river kept overflowing its banks. It was time to move, preferably to higher ground.

After talking with the Fayu and doing some exploring, we found the perfect spot. About half an hour upriver, there was a small hill. The Fayu suggested that we move there, saying that it wasn't far from the river. The idea of having a nice breeze, fewer mosquitoes and a 360-degree view convinced us.

So Papa went with the Fayu to scope out the land. He came back delighted. A few weeks later, four friends from America arrived and volunteered to help us build the new house. Time and flooding had also destroyed the Fayu's huts, so they decided to rebuild the village around the site of our new house. Soon, wood chips filled the air.

However, when a Fayu says that something isn't far from the river, one can't necessarily believe him or her. What they considered 'not far' was still a long way from our definition of 'close'. Anticipating a short walk from the river to our new house, we left the boat and started up the path. Or more accurately, intended to start up the path. The forest here was situated in a swamp. A particular tree, the swamp palm, was prevalent in this area and posed a real complication for us, since they are covered with long, sharp thorns.

'And how are we supposed to get through that?' I asked Papa.

'Walk,' he said, without batting an eyelash.

'Walk? On what? There is no ground.'

'Sabine, have you gotten soft?' Papa laughed. 'Don't you see the log over there?'

I walked to where he was pointing and skeptically looked at the narrow log that sat barely higher than the water level.

'Don't worry, Sabine. I'll watch out that you don't fall,' Ohri said, joining in Papa's laughter.

With wounded pride, I replied, 'No. I'll be fine.' I picked up what I could carry and began the trek. But walking through the swamp isn't an easy thing. The 'path' up to the hill consisted of logs that had been laid end to end through the swamp. Many of them were narrow, and all of them were slippery. If you started to slip, you couldn't hold onto anything, since most of the available trees were the thorny swamp palms. And the many times I did slip off the logs, I sank in the mud almost as quickly as through water.

Further adding to the fun were the thousands of insects lying in wait. During one of these crossings, I was covered head to toe in black spiders and even had to shake a scorpion out of my sleeve.

But in the end, the trek was a lot of fun. I loved the feeling of adventure. And if I was lucky, the area would be flooded and we could paddle by canoe through the swamp to the base of the hill.

The way through the swamp was about 800 yards. Once through, it took an additional thirty minutes to walk up the hill to the house. That part of the trek was rather pleasant. The flora and fauna that lined the pathway were quite impressive. The huge trees provided comfortable shade and were filled with countless varieties of birds.

The top of the hill offered an indescribable view. Three hundred and sixty degrees of pure jungle for as far as the eye could see – like an emerald carpet that spread around us for hundreds of square miles. I fell in love with the place at first sight. Our new house was located on top of paradise.

And at the peak of the hill stood our new, two-storey house. The lower floor was one big room to be used as a kitchen, dining and living area. On the left side of the room was a small bathroom, and next to it a narrow set of stairs led to the top floor. There were three rooms on that floor: one for Mama and Papa, one for Christian, and one for Judith and me to share.

A quiet period followed as our old routine was soon reestablished. In the meantime, I had turned fifteen years old but still enjoyed the company of my childhood friends. In our absence, they had grown to be young men. Even Ohri, once small and lame, had become a big, confident man. My heart filled with sisterly love as I watched him. I thought about the time when he almost died of infection and how he had come to be a close family member. Now he sat there, grinning up at me, repeating over and over how much he had missed us. His tears had been replaced by joy. 'My family is with me again.'

But slowly I became aware that the feeling of things being the same as always was an illusion. We had changed. We didn't play our crazy games any more. No more 'hunt the crocodile'. No more fire-building or hunts for small animals. The distance of our house from the river didn't bother me now. But it would have once upon a time. The childhood Sabine would have hated being that far from a good swim.

I was more interested in other things now, like the lives of the Fayu women. I slowly wandered from the world of boys into the world of women and found myself spending more and more time in their company. We sat around in groups, went fishing together, made sago and looked after the small children. I think this was difficult for Tuare. He often sat near us, watching everything I did, and seemed unhappy with what he saw. He wasn't in love with me; I had always perceived that I was neither male nor female to him. I think he simply wanted the young Sabine back, and suddenly I had grown up.

That I hadn't been 'stolen' yet was a constant source of wonder for the Fayu. By their standards, I was getting rather old to still be unmarried. But it never occurred to the Fayu men to touch either Judith or me. When my father once asked them about it, they said, 'You stay with your skin, and we'll stay with ours.' We were simply from a different world.

When I once asked Judith about this, she laughed and said, 'They wouldn't know what to do with us anyway. We're not good at harvesting sago, catching fish or weaving nets. The men are afraid that they wouldn't eat if they married us. So they would rather marry a woman who fits their needs. And Sabine, I can't imagine you holding your tongue if you disagreed with something. Or quietly sitting with the women while the men go hunting.'

I had to laugh at the image of being a wife to a Fayu warrior, but today I'm not so sure. Maybe the idea isn't so unthinkable. Maybe I could have adapted to being a tribal woman. I think that my life might have been easier had I stayed with the Fayu. Certainly it would have been less complicated than what I've experienced during my years in the West. But back then, I didn't concern myself too much with these issues. I was simply glad to be back with the Fayu and to have regained a part of my heart.

We would sit around the campfire in the evening with the setting sun at our backs. It was cooler than being down at the river. A light wind wafted over us, and often I could watch the lightning playing on the horizon. The young men would tell their stories – usually about hunting or women. I often had to laugh to myself. Men really are the same everywhere. Once, while Bebe explained to me that he wanted a woman with large breasts, he stood up and demonstrated the desired dimensions.

'Bebe,' I laughed, 'such big breasts don't exist here.'

'Do they exist where you come from?' he asked with an interested expression.

'Yes, but they aren't real,' I answered.

'Aren't real?' Confusion played across the boys' faces. As they all looked at me expectantly, I regretted having said anything. The explanation is too complicated, too far removed from anything they would understand. It was simply too different.

'Forget it,' I said.

Another major change that had occurred in our absence was that the base in Danau Bira had been closed down.

There weren't enough foreign families left to maintain it. So now we had to travel between Foida and the capital city of Jayapura, where we had rented a house.

Also, a high school had been built there – Hillcrest International School – which we now attended, along with forty other foreigners. For us kids this meant that we spent more and more time in the city and could only visit the Fayu during vacations. Jayapura was the place where my two worlds touched – a bit of jungle and a bit of civilization.

One day shortly before the end of a vacation in Foida, I became aware that this feeling of being 'between' – not really a clear part of either world – was the primary feeling of my life. And this was a problem.

The rest of the family had all ready left for the city, while I stayed behind with Papa to enjoy a last few days with the Fayu. Papa asked if I felt like going on a trip. Naturally I did, and so we began on our way to the Sefoidi clan. Tuare was waiting down by the boat to join us on the journey. I sat next to him at the front of the boat and helped him with his job of watching for floating logs, debris and sunken sandbanks.

It was lovely on the river – sun on my face, nature all around and sweetness in the air. Since Mama wasn't there, Tuare gave me some sugarcane. We ripped off the hard outer skin with our teeth and sucked out the juice. Lips smacking and juice running down our arms, soon we were covered in stickiness. But no worries – a dip in the river would easily take care of that.

A wonderful peace came over me, one that was increasingly elusive. The jungle was still a place of magic for me – my home. But I had the feeling that this home was slipping through my fingers. I tried to hold onto it with all my strength, but it just kept slipping away. I no longer knew who

I was or where I belonged. The time I had spent in the West had influenced me more than I had been willing to admit. I felt torn between the desire to remain a child of the jungle and the lure of becoming a modern woman. A decision was going to have to be made, sooner rather than later.

Tuare snapped me out of my thoughts by shaking my arm and pointing to a large tree on the shore. I quickly saw what he intended – there were thousands of black shapes hanging off the branches.

'Do you remember? Didn't they taste good?' Tuare asked.

'Oh yes!' I softly breathed, more to myself than to him.

Suddenly the shapes moved, and the sky was covered with bats. As I watched them flying overhead, I had to ask myself why I was thinking so much. After all, this was my home, my family. Everything was as it always had been and always would be. At least that's what I wanted to believe. A few days later, vacation was over, and I returned to Jayapura.

My feeling of dislocation continued during the next vacation with the Fayu. All my friends were there to greet me, which made me happy, but even they seemed to sense that something was wrong. And they didn't know what to do about it. Since I didn't know either, I decided to simply repress my growing uneasiness. I concentrated on living my life as though nothing was wrong, as if the joys of childhood continued without interruption.

35

THE BABY WITHOUT
A NAME

Even though my feeling of separation from the tribe was painful, it did have a useful consequence. We had grown up so immersed in the Fayu culture that we were simply part of it. Now I could take a more objective look at their culture and customs. This became evident during a fishing trip with Fusai.

Fusai had woven a net from bark and invited me to join her. I followed her through the jungle to the stream she had in mind. Fusai walked into the water and laid out her net. A short time later, it was full of fish.

When we returned to the village, a stirred-up Tuare was waiting for me. He said that a woman had come to our house with a very sick baby. Mama wasn't there, so they were asking for my help. I took the baby in my arms, a small girl not more than a few months old. She had a high fever. What should I do?

I decided to do the obvious first – a bath, as the child was covered in dirt. I filled a large bowl full of warm water. But as I went to pick up the baby, her father stepped in. He was afraid because he didn't understand what I was planning to do with the child. It occurred to me that the Fayu never washed their babies; the river is too cold for that.

'I won't hurt your baby,' I tried to explain. 'Just the opposite. The dirt is bad for her.'

He didn't seem to agree. 'That's dangerous,' he said aggressively, pointing at the water.

'No,' I disagreed. 'Feel it.'

Carefully he dipped his hand in the water and seemed surprised when he felt its warmth. After much back and forth, he finally gave me permission to bathe his child; the mother had been agreeable from the beginning.

Bystanders gathered around and watched this new procedure. I lay the sick baby into the water, which she seemed to enjoy, since she immediately calmed down. Behind me I heard the occasional 'Oh' and 'Ah'. My public was enthusiastic. After the bath, I wrapped the baby in a dry towel and gave her back to her mother. I asked if the baby had been named yet. 'No,' I was told, 'she doesn't have any teeth.'

The next morning, the mother came to our house to show me that the baby was eating again and had no fever. I went happily through the day and fell asleep more satisfied than I had been in a long time.

But when I woke the next day, the news reached me that the baby died during the night. I sat in bed and cried, crushed by the responsibility. Why didn't I do more? Had I done something wrong? I felt so helpless, so powerless. When I was younger, my view of death and dying was consistent with that of the Fayu. It was a natural occurrence and not a matter of profound grief. So why did this death hit me so hard?

I found myself in a new place now. My time in the West

had exposed me to a different view – one that said that death was preventable, that illness could be controlled. Yet I had been unable to save the baby. Fierce anger arose in me.

I went outside, where Papa was all ready waiting. The mother was holding her dead baby in her arms, singing the Fayu song of mourning. It astonished me to hear her mourn for the baby because, according to their old customs, they did not mourn a child that died before it had teeth. This was another small change we noticed over the years.

Later that day, I went with Ohri to watch the burial. We came upon a clearing where the father had built a death hut. The Fayu had given up keeping corpses in their own huts. Instead, they now built high platforms out in the forest. Four long beams were driven into the ground, and a small platform was lashed to the top of them. I noticed two long arrows protruding from the ground and asked Ohri what their purpose was.

'The arrows help the spirits to find the dead.'

I watched the mother lay her baby on the platform. Next to the body she placed the child's only possession: the towel in which I had wrapped her.

Tears ran down my cheeks. I felt horrible. Ohri grabbed my hand and whispered, 'Don't be sad, little sister. I will never leave you.' I gripped his hand tightly, glad for his company.

Papa later explained to me what the mourning ritual was – why they sometimes mourned for only a few days and other times for months. The Fayu told him that if the child was young, they only mourned a short time. 'We never gathered food with it. We didn't eat together or have any conversations. We did not share many memories with a small child.'

In the Fayu culture, the length of mourning is related to the age of the deceased. The older the dead person was, the longer they mourned. When a tribe elder died, the mourning could last for weeks. The bones that remained were hung up in the huts as we might hang photographs. Often I would visit someone's hut and be proudly introduced to the skulls with the words, 'This is my uncle. This is my grandfather, and over here is my sister.'

It may seem macabre to us in the West, but this was the Fayu way of remembering their loved ones.

36

THE BEAUTY AND THE BEAST

The view from our hill was a constant source of joy and wonder to me. It gave you the impression that you were on top of the world. And almost every evening, we enjoyed a stunning sunset. Sometimes I could watch the fog rise out of the jungle. It seemed mysterious and mighty. Stronger than the millions of giant trees, it buried them without effort.

I woke up one morning with the feeling that there was something special about the day. I climbed out of bed and crept downstairs. The rest of the world was still sleeping. I went into the kitchen to prepare my coffee as usual but was startled when I looked out the window. The ground was covered in white.

I put down the coffeepot and ran to the door. A grand view met my eyes. Above me there was blue sky, and on the horizon, the rising sun sent its golden rays beaming my way. But more striking than either of those was the fact that the ground wasn't visible. Thick fog covered the entire jungle and our hill. I could barely see my feet, so I took a careful step, and then another.

I was standing on a cloud like I had dreamed about doing as a child, and it felt amazing. I was on top of the world – thrilled beyond words. This scene would last for ever in my mind. Basking in the moment, I stood there until the sun burned away the fog.

I finally went back into the house, finished making coffee, and sat on the stairs outside. *Yes,* I thought to myself, *this is it. This is the place where I can be happy.* But immediately following that thought, I was overcome by a wave of sorrow. Why had my dream of standing on the clouds been fulfilled at this moment in time? It came just as I was feeling that I didn't belong here any more.

I thought back to my time in Germany and my grand-mother in Bad Segeberg. I remember how good the German coffee smelled in comparison to the instant brew I held in my hands. And the bread! How I missed the German breakfast rolls, thickly covered in a chocolate spread. I remembered the cool weather and our walks around the lake.

Then I felt guilty. Here I was, yearning for my parents' homeland, when nature just shared with me an experience I had long yearned for. No. I had no right to be homesick. No right to long for a strange land. This was my home; this was where I belonged.

Was nature trying to remind me of something? Were its wonders being displayed to keep me bound to it for ever? A friend always remains a friend and never leaves the other behind. That was the rule I had learned from the Fayu.

Not long after this experience, I woke up unexpectedly in the middle of the night. Something was wrong. I listened but could only hear silence. The jungle was completely still – an indication of danger. I sat up in my bed, still bleary-eyed.

Then I heard a sound that was reminiscent of the ocean. It grew closer and louder, turning into a roar. Fear blossomed within me. The sound kept coming, and suddenly everything was shaking. The floor, the walls, my bed. I pulled the blanket over my head, sure the house was about to collapse. It seemed like an eternity before quiet returned.

I knew immediately that this had been an earthquake. I had experienced quite a few of them before, but never one this powerful. The jungle seemed to have become a mighty rushing ocean, undulating with wave after wave. This singular event left me shaken.

And again I had the feeling that the jungle didn't want to let me go. First, the soft, gentle fog and now this display of elemental power. The jungle was making sure it wasn't forgotten. That I didn't only see it but also felt it in my bones.

The next morning, I asked Papa if he had felt the earthquake. 'What earthquake?' he asked. 'I must have slept through it.' It felt like the earthquake of the century to me, and he didn't even notice it. Clearly, this had been a message meant for me.

37

BISA AND BEISA

O ne evening, we learned the Fayu creation story. Kloru, the father of Tuare and Bebe, is the one who told us the legend. He is one of the best storytellers I've ever met.

'There once was a large village with many people who all spoke the same language,' Kloru began. We were sitting around the campfire that evening, waiting for the pork to finish cooking. Kloru spoke in a language that I couldn't understand at all. I asked Papa about it, and he excitedly explained that Kloru was speaking in an ancient dialect once used by his ancestors. To make sure he didn't miss anything, Papa recorded the story on a cassette player. Papa's language skills were good enough that he was able to make sense of the old dialect and translate it for me.

> *These people lived in peace. But one day, a great fire came from the sky, and suddenly there were many languages. Each language was only spoken by one man and one*

woman, who could communicate only with one another and not with anyone else.

So they were spread out over the earth. Among them were a man and a woman named Bisa and Beisa. They spoke in the Fayu tongue. For days they travelled, trying to find a new home. One day, they arrived at the edge of the jungle, and it began to rain. The rain wouldn't stop. Days and weeks it rained, and the water kept rising.

Bisa and Beisa built themselves a canoe and collected many animals that were trying to escape from the water. As they paddled, they kept repeating, 'Rain, stop! Thunder, stop! We are scared.'

But the rain wouldn't stop. The water rose until it covered all the trees. Everything died in the flood. Everything except for Bisa, Beisa and the animals in their canoe.

They had given up all hope when, days later, they suddenly came upon land. Bisa, Beisa and the animals got out of the boat and found themselves on top of a small hill. Before them they saw a cave leading into the earth. They crawled inside its cover, feeling great relief.

Soon afterward, it stopped raining, and the water disappeared. The animals swarmed into the jungle, but Bisa and Beisa stayed in the cave. They built themselves a home and had children, who themselves had children until they became a great tribe known as the Fayu.

Bisa and Beisa still live there today but no longer in human form. They immortalized themselves by turning into stone.

Have you seen the stones in the cave? Back to back they sit.
And when we have problems, we go to them and tell them
about it.

How interesting, I thought to myself. *So strange, and yet so*
familiar. People really do share a common history. I glanced around
the dark jungle, imagining what it must have been like for
Bisa and Beisa, all alone in a canoe on the cold water. *They*
must have felt so lost, I thought, and scooted closer to Ohri.

38

REVERSE GEAR

Even more surprising than the story Kloru told us was the fact that Tuare had never heard it himself. He knew about the stone figures, Bisa and Beisa, but until Papa asked about it, he had never heard the legend behind them. I always tend to remember this whenever I think about the development of the Fayu culture. How could such a vibrant culture have gotten to the point where it stopped developing and began regressing?

One of the acknowledged signs that a people or culture is on the verge of extinction is that knowledge no longer gets transmitted from generation to generation. I still have trouble believing that no Fayu remembered the white visitors they received in the 1940s. The memory of the Dutchmen had apparently been lost within a generation.

It's not as if they didn't have time to tell each other stories. Men would often spend the majority of the day sitting around doing just that. But knowledge that takes a lifetime to acquire was not being shared. The next generation always had to start from the ground up. And over time, they lost the desire for any knowledge beyond what was needed to survive.

The circumstances in which the Fayu lived – cut off from outside cultural influences – added to this pattern of regression. The only foreign tribes of which the Fayu were aware were the Kirikiri and the Dou. But because of the constant warfare, the tribes, and therefore the cultures, didn't mingle. They didn't acquire any new knowledge or develop ideas for how to improve their lives. And no one intervened in their culture.

I occasionally get asked if it wouldn't have been better to leave these 'noble savages' alone in their paradise. This might have kept them from being exposed to corrupting influences. I answer by making the observation that it is not 'paradise' to live in a culture so stuck in its destructive traditions that the people are killing each other to the point of extinction. How is it 'paradise' when children live in constant fear and terror? This paradise had been on the verge of turning into a living hell.

Should we really have left the Fayu to their fate once we learned of the danger they faced? Our contact with them served as a gentle push from the outside that prompted them to find a better way of doing things. Contact with other cultures was, in the end, unavoidable, because they would have been exposed to the outside world at some point.

The better question is whether our living with them has left them more prepared to deal with those encounters. It was one of our goals to be a bridge between the Fayu and the prevailing cultures so that when contact did occur, the shock would be minimized, and they would be well prepared. In the end, this would actually give them a greater chance of retaining their culture.

39

IT IS NOT GOOD FOR
MAN TO BE ALONE

When we first moved to the Fayu, we wondered whether they knew any songs, since we never heard them singing. This question was answered fairly quickly. We had just returned from Danau Bira, and our things had once again been stolen. As we were cataloguing our losses, we heard singing from the other side of the river. It was Nakire singing in a lovely monotone.

'Ohhhhhhh,' he sang. 'The Fayu are like birds. Ohhhh, they always take from the same tree. Ohhhh, such bad people. Ohhhh, poor Klausu, poor Doriso. They are so sad and wonder where their stuff is. Ohhh . . .'

Papa was delighted as it became clear to us that the Fayu simply improvise a song to match their situation. The songs only consist of three notes with which they express whatever they are feeling in the moment. It is not the most sophisticated music, but it is a sound I quickly came to love.

Their use of songs to express themselves may be one of

the reasons the Fayu do not seem to suffer from depression or other psychological disorders. Feelings are immediately expressed. There are even times set aside for the release of emotions, for example, the mourning song. When the song of mourning runs its course, the grieving truly is finished, and life resumes as normal.

When a person experienced a traumatic event, he might lie for weeks in his hut, not saying a word but singing for hours at a time. During this period, other clan members would provide him with food. Then one day, he would simply get up with the trauma behind him. Cleansed of pain, he would smilingly resume his everyday tasks.

As we were shuttling back and forth between Jayapura and Foida, it frequently happened that the family would be split between the two sites. Papa had a difficult time being separated from Mama. He missed her and gave the impression of feeling lost without her.

That was his state one evening as he sat at the top of our hill. Mama had stayed behind in Jayapura because Christian had malaria again. The Fayu had all ready gone to their huts, and I sat in the house, reading by flashlight.

All of a sudden I heard odd sounds outside the house. I looked out and saw Papa standing there, singing a familiar three-toned mourning song in Fayu. 'Ohhh, Doriso. Where are you, Doriso? I am so alone. Ohhh. Chief Kologwoi has a wonderful wife and so does Nakire. Ohhh, only I am alone. Ohhh, my heart is heavy.'

I could barely keep from laughing. My father really can be amusing sometimes. But he had barely begun the second verse when the Fayu came out of their huts. They hugged him and tried to comfort him and then joined him in his mourning. 'Ohhh, Doriso, come quickly.

Ohhh, Doriso, your husband needs you. Ohhh, Doriso, he is so sad. Ohhh, Doriso, come quickly.' And so it rang out into the night. It was a touching sound that I will never forget.

Ohri came by to visit the next morning. He wanted to show me something. I followed him to the edge of the village, where he showed me a freshly built hut. 'My new house,' he said, full of pride. I admired it effusively as is the Fayu custom. I assured him I had never seen such a nice hut. His entire face beamed.

The hut was built simply but had obviously been constructed with much love and care. The roof was covered with the usual palm branches and, more unusually, the hut had walls. Simple stairs led up to the entrance. But what really touched me was the fact that Ohri had decorated his hut – a rarity among the Fayu. The floor had been covered with bamboo strips, except for the spot in the middle that was intended as a place for the fire.

I smiled to myself as I realized that Ohri had marriage on his mind. *Ohri will surely make a good husband,* I thought with a bit of jealousy. But I was proud of him. He had suffered so much in his life and yet had still become a tower of support for me and many others. Whenever I didn't feel well, it was always Ohri who sat next to me and held my hand. It was his presence more than all others that brought me some of the peace I was looking for. He had become an important part of my life and was one of the reasons I clung to life in the jungle. In this moment, I realized with great clarity how important Ohri was to me as a friend and brother.

Together we walked back to my house. I offered Ohri a cup of tea, but like all other Fayu, he simply wrinkled his nose and said, 'Hau'. We sat together in silence on the log outside my house and admired the scenery. For a moment, I felt completely at peace. I didn't have to think about the future or what it held for me. My thoughts turned to Ohri. I wished him the best that life could offer.

40

INFIDELITY AND OTHER PROBLEMS OF LIFE

As with most crimes, infidelity among the Fayu was once punishable by death. But times had changed. The Fayu's ability to find new ways to solve their problems continued to amaze us. Papa tried to stay out of tribal politics. The Fayu needed to make their own decisions, because we were not there to rule, but serve.

And so I stood at the edge of the village and watched a man and woman sitting in the middle of the clearing. Their hands were tied. They'd had an affair with one another despite being married to other people.

I looked on curiously to see what would happen. First, Chief Kologwoi gave a speech in which he said that the two people had done something wrong. He talked and talked for what seemed like an eternity. And even though he stopped talking eventually, the process was far from over. Next, Nakire stood up and gave an equally long speech saying essentially the same thing as Chief Kologwoi. The burning sun rose overhead. Various tribal members gave speeches, all confirming what had been said and condemning the infidelity.

Finally, in late afternoon, it was time for Chief Kologwoi to announce their punishment. I had become quite thirsty and hungry by this time. It keeps surprising me how long the Fayu can go without water. I felt especially sorry for the two tied up on the ground, who didn't even have the option of getting water. They never lifted their shame-filled eyes from the ground during the entire procedure.

Chief Kologwoi stood up; he had reached a decision. He declared that the two would have to make restitution. Each of them would have to give gifts to the spouse of the person they had cheated with. This would go on until the spouse was satisfied. The guilty man brought the husband knives, arrows and a pig until the wronged man indicated his satisfaction. The guilty woman gave sago, netting and other items to the wronged wife.

Infidelity was very rare in the jungle. I asked Papa if there was love in Fayu marriages. 'I don't know,' he answered honestly. 'Except with Nakire and Fusai, I haven't really seen a lot of evidence of loving marriages. They never hug or kiss in public. When I ask the men to put an arm around their wives so I can take a picture, they giggle and act like shy children.'

I thought back to the times I had seen a Fayu man shooting his wife out of anger. All of this indicated to me that the Fayu married more for survival than for love. And sexuality is handled very discreetly. When a man had stolen a woman to be his wife, they simply disappeared into the jungle for several days until she accepted him as husband.

'So what does a man do who has several wives and wants to sleep with one of them?' I continued to question Papa.

'He would just take her into the jungle. But polygamy has

pretty much died out. The older men who used to take young girls as second or third wives have decided to let the younger men have them.'

A wise decision, I thought. With more young women available, competition was decreased, and kidnappings became fewer, which produced less need for revenge and war.

But it was hard for me to imagine a culture in which there was no love between husbands and wives. I had seen several movies during my stay in America that dealt with love, emotions and sex. Those topics couldn't be limited to the western world, could they? Besides, Mama and Papa were happy together, though of course they did have the same goal in life and loved what they did. All of these issues spun around in my fifteen-year-old brain. In the end, I was simply glad that I was too young to be considering marriage.

Chief Kologwoi looked at the assembled restitution items and asked the wronged parties if they were satisfied. They indicated that they were, and the matter was settled – forgiven and forgotten.

Infidelity in the Fayu culture is a serious matter. We never heard of an affair that lasted. They were always quickly ended and never rekindled. I think such strict rules are necessary when one lives in such a contained environment. The close quarters in which the Fayu existed demanded that they work cooperatively to put aside grievances and complaints; otherwise, they would self-destruct as a community.

Many thoughts ran through my head as I lay in bed that night. I kept thinking about the future and what love had in store for me. The fact that I wasn't sure how to deal with my emotions only served to complicate matters. My Fayu heritage had a very different set of rules for this than did my western heritage. Since I didn't know to which world I belonged, I didn't know which cultural rules regarding emotion and love applied to me.

I had entered the eleventh grade and was preparing to continue my studies after graduation. To do that, I would have to return to the 'civilized' world. But the jungle was the place where I felt most at home. Or was it? Life there had changed – mostly for the good, as Chief Kologwoi's solution indicated – and I found myself yearning for something indefinable, something that seemed out of reach there. On the one hand, I wanted the quiet life that the jungle offered. But on the other hand, there were possibilities that simply could never be realized there. How could I get a college education in the jungle? How could I find a husband? How could I fit into a place that no longer fit me?

After all, wasn't I German? A white girl with white parents? My skin was clearly white, but what was I on the inside? Who was I, really?

41

THE DAY THAT OHRI
DIED

Whenever school holidays were approaching and a return to the jungle became imminent, my heart did a happy dance. Dark thoughts of the future faded away for a while.

We had flown to Kordesi and were motoring upriver in our aluminium boat. Christian and I sat at the front in the lookout position. We had forgotten to put on sunblock, as teenagers are prone to do. When we arrived in the village, I didn't feel anything yet, but by the next morning, my sunburn was so painful that I could barely move.

Christian and I had both burned our backs very badly. In some places, my skin turned black and fell off in strips. Mama reprimanded us; our pain-contorted expressions elicited no pity from her. Had we known the tragedy that was approaching us, we would never have given our sunburn a second thought. In fact, it is a wonder that I remember it at all, given the intensity of what was about to follow.

Over the next few days, Mama noticed that Ohri hadn't come to visit us yet. 'I'll go down to the village and ask where he is,' I said. But my inquiries were fruitless. *He must have stolen a wife,* I thought to myself with a grin. Later that day, I heard a voice call out. It was Ohri.

I jumped up and went toward the village to greet him. Mama was running ahead of me; she had noticed that something was wrong. I looked past Mama and saw Ohri. He was very thin and pale. Ohri approached us with weak, halting steps. Then he collapsed. Suddenly, everything moved as though in a nightmare. I was no longer part of the events but watched from a foggy distance.

I stood helplessly at the edge of the village and watched Mama place Ohri's head in her lap, softly stroking his cheek. I took no notice of the things around me – of Christian standing on top of the hill, of Papa running to Mama. I only saw Ohri, motionless in the grass.

Mama bent down to him as he said something to her. She whispered in his ear and he smiled weakly. Suddenly a quiver went through his body and then he stopped moving. Ohri was dead.

I have seldom seen Mama cry. But sitting on the ground with Ohri in her arms, the tears began to flow. I sank to the ground. It seemed as though time stood still. Nothing moved – not birds, or wind or leaves. I sat there and cried. I had lost my brother – the one who had survived so much calamity. The ground had been pulled out from under my feet, and I began to fall.

Ohri died of tuberculosis – a Western disease to which he had been exposed by a Dani man. He had made his way to us to see us one more time. This is what he told Mama right before he died.

It was a black day for us. A day I'd rather not remember.

Ohri, who had promised to stay with me for ever, was dead. Everything seemed to lose meaning. Everything I had clung to was gone.

That evening, I stared into the flames that consumed Ohri's hut – the hut he had built with such love and hope – along with everything else that had belonged to him. With tears in my eyes, I watched a part of my life go up in flames. The fire took a piece of my heart with it. Ohri, who had survived so much, who was so brave and strong and always full of life – why did he have to die? Ohri had believed so strongly in life. He wanted to marry and start a family. He had been my rock, and he would never come back.

Headaches plagued me for days, and I began having a recurring nightmare. In it, I saw Ohri burning along with his hut, flames wrapping around his body. I heard him screaming and crying for help and kept trying to save him. But I couldn't reach him and had to watch as he burned. The nightmare returned night after night. Each time, I tried to save him without success.

On a Wednesday afternoon not long afterward, I was in bed trying to sleep, since nightmares from the previous night had left me weary. The humidity seemed unbearable. My throat tightened, and it became harder to breathe.

No! No! No! the protests rang in my head. But I couldn't open my mouth. It had become too dry. I was trying to save Ohri again, but this time the flames were coming toward me. As the flames approached, I felt my hand beginning to burn. Terror rose up within me and I screamed. I thrashed around like a wild animal trying to extinguish the flames. My whole body was in agony, but I kept fighting.

Then I felt a pair of cool arms surround me and hold me tight. From far away I could hear Mama's voice. 'Sabine, Mama is here. Just hold onto me. It will be over soon.' She kept comforting me until my screaming turned into uncontrollable sobbing. We sat like that until it became dark outside.

'I can't stay here any more,' I whispered to Mama.

'I know,' she answered sadly.

As she gently stroked the wet hair out of my face, I heard my father's voice next to me. I hadn't noticed that he had joined us. 'Uncle Edgar has offered to pay for you to go to a boarding school in Switzerland. Do you want to do that?' I nodded wordlessly.

Everything had suddenly and completely changed; my entire outlook was different. I did not realize this at the time. My only conscious thought was of my desire to flee as far and as fast as possible from these nightmares. I needed to get away from the flames, away from the pain, away from this world. Simply away. As much as the prospect of a new life scared me, I was determined to go, ready to move to the other side of the world by myself.

I gazed one last time over the unending jungle. I looked at the mighty trees forming green waves all the way to the horizon. I listened to the birdsong, the chirping of the insects, and took a deep breath of the tropical air. With one look back, I walked down the hill.

Behind me the mourning song of my tribe rose into the air. The Fayu watched as the little girl who had come to them so many years before now left them. They cried and mourned, singing to me that they loved me and that I should stay. Tuare stood at the front, and I could hear his faithful, familiar voice rise in mourning.

'Oh, my sister, oh why are you leaving me?'

I kept walking, tears running down my face. And so at the end of 1989, I left the jungle of West Papua, Indonesia.

My sister had left the previous year to study art in

England. Shortly after I left, Christian would also leave to go to school in Hawaii. And so our life together came to an end. As a family, we had gone through thick and thin, had played together, fought together and told each other stories. We had always loved each other. And now this life was broken. Broken by our growing up, broken by the losses we suffered. A part of my life was gone for ever.

42

MY NEW TRIBE

I dreamed. Flames surrounded me, intent on devouring me. I heard Ohri's screams and wanted to save him but couldn't get through. A pain-filled face, a hand stretching out for help. Then everything collapsed, and I saw only ash on the ground. It kept getting colder; everything was dark. I searched for warmth, for light. Panic rose as I desperately gasped for air. It was cold. So cold.

I awoke with a start and for a moment didn't know where I was. I looked at the darkness around me. Then memory came flooding back: the flight to Germany, the confusing train station, and the train on which I now travelled en route to Switzerland.

Shivering, I wrapped my coat more tightly around myself. The landscape streamed past as it became light outside. I was lucky. My first day as a European would be a sunny one.

A few hours later, I arrived at my destination. Friends of my parents picked me up at the central train station in

Zurich and drove me to the boarding school in Montreux. My excitement grew as we arrived at Lake Geneva.

I had read and re-read the information packet the school had sent, studying the pictures in great detail. It was a boarding school for girls and also a finishing school. I was supposed to graduate from high school here as well as learn how to behave in proper society. 'So you can become a true lady,' my uncle had said, probably meaning that it was time for me to lose my jungle manners.

Lake Geneva lay before us in all its majesty. Houses covered the shores and the hills that led up to the surrounding mountains. The sun shone brightly, and for the first time since my arrival in Europe, I began to feel a little better.

Soon I stood in front of the boarding school – a small, grey castle directly on the lakefront. 'Château Beau Cèdre' the sign said – my new home. A large door looking like something out of the Middle Ages swung open with a creak. A young lady welcomed us in French. I couldn't understand a word and so just smiled and nodded.

She led us to the entrance hall, where a wide staircase swept upward. I felt as if I was dreaming. Everything was so elegant and luxurious. I had never seen anything like it. Thick carpet covered the floor; old oil paintings hung on the walls. The furniture looked so expensive that I didn't dare sit on it, so I stood instead, awestruck at my new environment.

All formalities were quickly taken care of, and I was shown to my new room. It was a large room with four beds, two of which had all ready been claimed by a German girl and an Australian. A doorway led out onto a balcony that had a lovely view of Lake Geneva.

It was like something out of a fairy tale. The sorrow, the jungle, the Fayu, my family – it all disappeared into the depths of my subconscious. I had arrived in a new and exciting world. There was so much to see and explore. I had the feeling of beginning the greatest adventure of my life.

That evening I sat in my bed, overwhelmed by the day's experiences. I was still plagued by headaches but was able to ignore them. I went out on the balcony and gazed at the blue water. An involuntary thought popped up. *I wonder what Tuare would think if he could see me now.*

The thought about Tuare saddened me, so I pushed it from my mind. *Stop it!* I chided myself. *I don't want to think about that any more. I want to forget everything. I am finally where I belong – after all, my skin is white, my hair is blond and my eyes are green. This is my new home; Europe is my heritage and my future.* I determined to learn everything I could about this new world. I wanted to become a European – wanted to think like one, act like one and look like one. This was my new tribe.

With this thought ringing in my head, I went to bed and slept without nightmares for the first time in weeks.

43

CHÂTEAU BEAU CÈDRE

I threw myself into Western life. Having been raised in one of the most primitive parts of the world, I now wanted to experience the sophistication of Switzerland.

Term hadn't officially begun yet, so there was time to explore Montreux. I went with a couple of the girls to a grocery shop. Something there caught my eye. I don't remember what it was, only that it cost ten Swiss francs. *Hmm,* I thought to myself. *That's too expensive.* So I went to the cashier and told her that I would pay her five francs for it. She just looked at me in confusion. The girls, who had all ready noticed that I was a bit different, came and pulled me away.

'What are you doing, Sabine?' they whispered.

'This price is too high. I'm bargaining it down,' I said, as if explaining something obvious.

'You can't do that. You have to pay what it says on the price tag.'

That made no sense to me. Bargaining is the most

normal thing in the world. In Indonesia, we always negotiated on price. 'So who determines what an item costs?' I asked.

That was the job of the shop owner, the girls told me. 'Well, that is clearly unfair,' came my response. 'He could set an obscenely high price and I would have to pay it.' The girls had no response for that.

I left the grocer's almost angry, feeling cheated somehow. Although I had been shopping before when we were on furlough, my parents had always paid, so I had never noticed how differently things were done here. I was soon to find that this was true of many aspects of life.

The next day I took a walk with two schoolmates along the Bord du Lac. As was done in the jungle, I gave a friendly greeting to everyone we passed. Some greeted back, while others just looked at me suspiciously. After a while, one of the girls asked how I had managed to meet so many people in the short time I'd been there. I looked at her in confusion and told her that I didn't know anyone outside the school.

'Then why are you greeting everyone?' she asked me.

'Because that's what you do,' I answered.

She laughed. 'Here, you only greet people you know.'

And so I learned another rule about Western life, even if I didn't understand it. The next time we passed a stranger, I determinedly said nothing. But then I felt guilty, as though I had been impolite and uncivilized. When people met in the jungle, they either exchanged greetings or arrows. I had learned there that every person is either friend or foe, so it was always safer to say hello.

When we returned that afternoon to the boarding school, my roommates had arrived: Leslie from Australia and Susanne from Germany. We hit it off immediately and talked late into the night. Thankfully, Leslie quickly noticed that I had much to learn and took me under her wing. Over the next several months, we became close friends.

A few days later, I received my first letter from Indonesia. Mail was distributed every day after lunch, every girl hoping to hear her name called. I went up to my room and ripped open Mama's letter – the only thread that still connected me to the jungle.

Oh daughter of the dawn, joy of my heart, you won't believe what happened to me. There I sat with the Fayu, under the blazing sun, writing you a long letter by the sweat of my brow. The next day we went to Jayapura and I discovered to my dismay that I had left the letter behind. In it, I gave you an extensive description of how a centipede bit Papa in the ear. It included a lovely description of how Papa jumped from the bed almost to the ceiling. With a jump like that, he would have been assured a gold medal in the next Olympics.

When Papa asked me the next day what I was thinking after he got bitten, I told him, 'I'm glad that it didn't bite me.' Even Papa had to laugh at that. I'm an honest person, as you know, so be honest with me, my dear. How are you? I miss you very much and wonder if I will ever get used to not having you around every day.

Smiling, I went back to the girls. With the centipede story, my mother had managed to bring a bit of the jungle to Switzerland. But Leslie just looked at me critically.

'What is it?' I asked.

'You really need a new haircut,' she stated. 'Yours looks really out of style. And your clothes! We'll have to do something about that.'

That afternoon we went out – first to the hairstylist, where I wanted to cry when I saw how short my new style was. But Leslie assured me that this was the fashion. And then onward we went to the clothing stores. Soon, I was dressed like my friends.

The headmistress of the school was amused by our undertaking, but I finally felt like I had arrived. I even got a new pair of boots, calf-height and pointy-toed, like cowboy boots. I was very proud of my new purchases.

As I had always done, every morning I took the boots and shook them out before putting them on. Susanne and Leslie watched me out of the corners of their eyes. 'Sabine, what are you doing?' they carefully asked one day. Finally, I could teach them something. I explained that poisonous insects like to hide in shoes, and it could be dangerous if you didn't shake them out first.

'Well . . . we don't really have dangerous insects here,' Susanne grinned.

I didn't believe her. I simply couldn't imagine finding no insects in my shoes. After several months of this, the girls tried a different approach. 'Sabine,' Leslie began, 'in the whole time you've been here, have you ever found an insect in your shoes?'

I thought about it and had to admit, much to my surprise, that I had not. 'Then tomorrow, why don't you try putting them on without shaking them out first,' she suggested.

The next morning, I thought about it for a moment, and then for the first time in memory, I simply put my shoes on. It was an odd sensation. I screwed my eyes shut, shoved my foot in, and waited for the sting. But nothing happened. I opened my eyes again, proud to have passed this test of bravery.

My dearest Sabine,

Life is so different here without you. Christian is now going to school in Hawaii. After he left, I walked through the empty house and asked myself how life could go on. For twenty years you three have been my life. For me, everything else took second place in my heart, even if those things took a lot of my time and effort.

Then one day I had THE idea. The Fayu children were sitting around again, bored – especially the older ones. I've been noticing for a while that a certain group of boys have withdrawn from their families and won't listen to anyone any more. Diro has become their leader. And so I thought I should open a Fayu school to give them something to do.

During the next visit to Jayapura, I bought notebooks, pencils, sketchbooks and coloured pencils – pretty much everything you need for a school. When I returned to the jungle, I called all the kids together, gave them a bit of soap, and told them to assemble in the morning at sunrise.

I expected them around nine o'clock, since most of them would have to travel up or down the river, cross the swamp and climb the hill. As you know, this takes at least an hour. But your poor mother had seriously miscalculated. It was barely light outside when I was woken by rather loud children's voices.

'Oh, no, Klaus Peter! That's not what I meant!'

'Well, my dear,' he answered, 'you forgot to tell them that the sun should be well up in the sky before they arrived.'

That was my first lesson in school administration. Having no other choice, I got up and prepared for my first lesson. I had them all stand in a row and told all the unmarried young men to step forward. That included Tuare – who keeps asking about you – Klausu Bosa, Diro, Bebe, Atara, Isori and Abusai. I had them sit in a group and told them they were 'Claas Tiga' (Class Three). I told them that they should come to school every morning, cleanly washed. They should leave home at sunrise but not arrive here at that point. The usually rowdy boys sat quietly and listened intently.

Then I divided the other children into two groups: 'Claas Satu' (Class One) for the youngest of them (ages five to seven), and 'Claas Dua' (Class Two) for the middle-aged group (eight to ten). They were all quite proud of their new titles. I heard them informing each other, 'I am Claas Satu,' or 'I am Claas Dua,' grinning the whole while. They were glad for the change of pace.

I assembled Claas Tiga on our new veranda: thirteen boys and two girls – Doriso Bosa and Fusai. You wouldn't recognize Doriso Bosa any more. She has grown into the prettiest Fayu girl around.

Why only two girls? I'm not sure, but as you know, girls tend to be in short supply. And besides, the older girls have to help their mothers harvest sago.

While class was in session, Papa put together some things for the students. Everyone got a piece of soap for their clothing and a piece for their bodies, a T-shirt, a pair of shorts, a sketchbook and a pencil. And so began our first school day.

We're going to Vevey to look around. Do you want to come?' Leslie asked me.

'Yes,' I answered, and so a group of us set off. To my surprise, we stopped at the bus stop. 'What's going on?' I asked apprehensively. 'I thought we were going to Vevey.'

'It's too far to walk, so we have to take the bus.'

I looked around nervously. 'What is it, Sabine?' Leslie asked.

'Leslie,' I whispered. 'I've never been on a bus. I don't know how to do it. I'm scared.' Leslie laughed and explained the basics. But it took me quite a while to get up the courage to get on the bus.

Traffic in all its forms was a big problem for me. I knew about cars, but in Jayapura, the cars drove very slowly because the streets were covered with potholes. Here, there were so many cars, and they drove so very fast. Every time I had to cross the street where there wasn't a traffic light, I would begin to sweat. I couldn't judge the speed of the cars and was terrified of getting run over.

One day we were standing on the pavement, cars racing by in both directions. A small gap appeared in the traffic, so my friends ran across the street. I stood there, petrified.

'Sabine, come on all ready,' the girls called out.

I looked up and down the street and saw cars and more cars. Five minutes later, I was still standing in the same spot. The fear was simply too great. The girls consulted with one another and kept coming up with new ideas for how to get me across the street. I didn't find any of them very appealing and so kept walking along my side of the street until I found a traffic light crossing. The girls learned from this experience that if they planned to cross the street with me, they would have to allow for extra time. City traffic scares me to this day.

But in some respects, I had an advantage over my friends. This became apparent when we got to the subject of table manners. The students nicknamed one of our teachers 'Madame Etiquette'. She taught us things such as how to dress, how to set a proper table for various functions, who gets greeted first, how to walk down stairs gracefully, and how to get out of a car when wearing a short skirt. As part of our lessons, Madame Etiquette would sit at various tables and critique our manners.

She shook her head at my pathetic attempts to eat elegantly and pronounced, 'Sabine, you will never be a proper lady. But you should be able to get by on your charm.'

I often didn't like the food we were served, not being familiar with many of the dishes. And so I just pushed the food around my plate with a fork, trying to figure out what it was. But every Friday, we had ice cream – a favourite dessert for most of the girls, including myself.

This is where I could use my background to an advantage. I quickly noticed that people in the West don't have strong stomachs. So shortly before we were served the ice cream, I would start telling stories about what the Fayu ate in the jungle. Or how they would keep their dead in their huts while the body decayed. By the end, I wouldn't just have my own portion of ice cream but that of several others as well. Soon, people began to avoid my table on Fridays. I enjoyed the excess ice cream as long as I could, until I was forbidden to tell any more jungle stories at the table.

Madame Etiquette was greatly amused by my ice cream strategy. She was of a ripe old age, had seen much and taught many girls. She later told me that I was one of a kind. During our third or fourth lesson with her, we were given a reading assignment. I had a question and so raised my hand.

'Sabine,' she said. 'You don't have to raise your hand. You can simply ask me. A lady doesn't raise her hand.'

'Okay,' I answered and started again. 'Madame Etiquette,' I began. Everyone froze in shocked silence.

'What? Why are you all looking at me like that?' I asked in confusion.

'Sabine,' our teacher said sternly, 'what is my name?'

'Madame Etiquette,' I answered with assurance.

Now all the students were shaking with laughter. Perplexed, I looked around. Even the dear Madame had trouble keeping a straight face.

'No, Sabine, that is definitely *not* my name,' she corrected me. Suddenly I realized that the girls only called her that behind her back. It hadn't occurred to anyone that I was unfamiliar with the student tradition of giving nicknames to teachers.

Madame told me her real name, which I promptly forgot. For me and the other girls, she was and remained Madame Etiquette. I just didn't call her that to her face. *That* would've been impolite.

In the meantime, Mama was struggling with issues in her school, too.

My dear Sabine,

Last week, we were able to move into the new school-house. A few volunteers constructed some simple benches, and we brought two folding tables from the coast. Papa even set up a water drum by the school where the students can wash off before class.

I've been strict from the first day on. The children have to understand that learning requires discipline. You know how your mother feels about these things . . .

I wrote every student's name in his or her notebook, which they were then allowed to take home as long as they brought it back the next day. I had to give them very explicit instructions about this, since they have never owned a notebook or pencil before and didn't know how to take care of them.

I gave coloured pencils to Claas Dua and had them draw circles, ovals and squares. The little ones are happily experimenting with their pencils. For the older class, I brought marbles from the city. I asked each student to count out five of them. All fifteen of the students simply reached into the jar and gave me a handful without counting. They only have numbers up to three and so didn't know what 'five' was. So they just gave me however much would fit into their hands, 'a handful' being their next highest number.

So, I started teaching them one to ten in Indonesian. After writing down the numbers in their notebooks, I had them copy the numbers over and over. After two days, they had all ready filled up a whole notebook. They kept going at that pace, so I've had to keep ordering more notebooks from town. I can only marvel at their diligence.

I've also noticed large differences in intelligence among the students. Abusai was so slow that I considered putting him back into Claas Dua, but the other boys of Claas Tiga came and begged me not to do it. 'All right,' I said, 'but you have to help him with his homework.'

I saw all of Claas Tiga later that day, sitting under my guava tree helping Abusai practise. The poor boy didn't have much choice. They wouldn't let him leave. And lo and behold, it didn't take long before he caught up with the others. He is still a very slow student, but I'll let him stay in Claas Tiga.

I could relate to problems with school. There was just so much that was completely new to me; for example, class schedules. I stared at the paper, trying to make sense of it. Every day was different, with one subject in the morning and a different one in the afternoon. And on top of that, each day entailed a different combination of classes.

It was so simple in the jungle, I thought to myself. *The same subjects every day, and I got to decide whether to start with maths or English.* The high school in Jayapura had taught more subjects than we had in the jungle, but the teachers didn't vary from class to class, and they provided plenty of support. Now I was on my own. I got scared. *How could I keep track of my schedule and remember so much schoolwork at the same time?*

A Westerner may have trouble understanding why a class schedule could create such panic in me. But up until this point, I had never had to keep a rigid schedule of any sort. In the jungle, the rule was that if I don't arrive today, I'll arrive tomorrow.

That night, I had another nightmare in which I lost my class schedule. I ran from room to room and desperately asked if I was in the right place. I did, in fact, forget a class once. I arrived late, sweating profusely, and got my head chewed off.

After the class, I gathered my resolve, went up to the teacher to apologise, and tried to explain my difficulty with the schedule. She ended up becoming my favourite teacher. This woman taught French, which came easily to me, since I had all ready learned so many other languages. And French is much easier than Fayu.

Meanwhile, Leslie and Susanne continued their attempts to civilize me. Part of that involved going to shoot pool at a bar in Montreux. I was delighted to learn this new game and was pretty good for a beginner. But soon I discovered another problem: in between games, the other girls would discuss subjects about which I knew nothing.

Who on earth were the Beatles? Who was George Michael? Or what about that other guy, Elton George? No, Elton John? I didn't know anything about movies, either. The only actor I knew was Tom Cruise. A friend who was visiting me in Indonesia showed me pictures of him, sighing that she loved him. That confused me; she didn't know him personally. How could she be in love with him? I didn't know about the concept of being a fan and being love-crazed from a distance. It took me a long time to figure out how that worked.

The first time I was invited to a 'cinema', I had to ask what that was. Leslie quickly pulled me aside and explained it to me, but I began to get the feeling that people thought I was a little slow. So I decided to do something about that. Every Monday, I went to the small shop near the school and bought a stack of magazines. After several weeks, the shop-keeper greeted me by name. I suspect I was her best customer.

I went back to my room and read all the magazines thoroughly, looking at the pictures and trying to memorize names and faces. But just when I thought I was caught up, something new would be added. It was very overwhelming. For example, I would just have learned the major rock groups, and then someone would ask, 'How can you not know who Boris Becker is?' I would sigh quietly, go back to my store and ask for the sports magazines. And then came politics. Musicals. Opera singers. And so on, and so on. Western culture seemed endless to me. But I had an iron will and didn't give up.

The wonders of technological communication scared me more than they delighted me. One day, while the mail was being given out, one of the girls was told that she had received a fax. *A fax? What was that?* I turned to Leslie, who had all ready taken a deep breath in anticipation. But this time, I didn't believe her explanation. It is not possible that you could feed a page into a machine and have it come out on the other side of the world. How is a piece of paper supposed to get through the telephone lines? I had roughly the same response when I saw my first mobile phone. It seemed like magic.

It slowly dawned on me how different this world was from the one in which I had grown up. A grain of doubt lodged itself in my determined heart. Was I really going to make it as a European? I felt lost and overwhelmed by the task. When I got another letter from Mama, I enjoyed another touch of 'normality'.

My dear Sabine,

There is so much to tell. Thankfully, the helicopter is coming today and can take this letter back with it. Here in Fayu country, it is sometimes hard to get a letter to you.

I still don't speak Fayu as well as your father, which causes great laughter in our school. But as long as I can point at objects or draw them on the blackboard, we do all right. But how am I supposed to communicate concepts like loyalty, trust, etc? It is always hard to figure out the Fayu word for abstract concepts.

Maths classes are going well, though. They've managed to grasp the marble exercise, whether I ask for three, four or six marbles. I go from student to student, repeating the same question until they get it. If one of them is having difficulty, I send him outside with another student to practise. Usually that works. Now they can tell the adults, 'Today I have seen four pigs.' Or they can excitedly go home and say, 'Afou (dad), our pig has had five piglets.' They then take their father's hand and count out the five fingers. The fathers are proud because their children can now do something the grown-ups cannot.

I've started teaching the alphabet to Claas Tiga. I'm still amazed that it only took them a week to learn the letters A through to J. Interestingly enough, the boys who had great difficulty with maths are much better with the alphabet. After the alphabet, I began teaching syllables. It actually didn't take that long for them to read and write their names.

Their excitement at learning the new concepts of reading and writing is delightful to watch. I am so proud of my students. Papa suggested starting a class for adults, but I'd rather teach the children, so someone else will have to be found for that. After all, I've known most of the kids since they were babies – almost as long as I've known my own children, who are now gallivanting around the world. I hope, dearest Sabine, that you are doing well and learning a lot.

'Sabine, do you know what a condom is?' Leslie, my 'life teacher', asked late one evening.

'Condensed milk?' I asked sleepily.

Leslie laughed. 'No, it's nothing to drink. You use a condom to have safe sex.'

'Safe sex? Can one have dangerous sex?' Now my interest had been awakened.

'Come, I'll show you,' she said and got a banana. Leslie ripped open a small square package, pulled out the opaque contents and stretched it over the banana. I watched with big eyes. Then she explained what the purpose of it was.

I took the dressed-up banana. 'But this is much bigger than a . . . you know. Wouldn't it just slip off?'

'Sabine, how many naked men have you seen in your life?' Leslie asked.

'Oh, quite a few,' I answered proudly and honestly. 'But none whom this would fit.'

'Well then, I think you're in for a surprise,' she laughed. I had to laugh, too. The poor banana just looked so silly.

That wasn't the only thing Leslie told me that evening about men and sex. I lay awake a long time that night and could barely believe what I'd been told. Mama hadn't mentioned all those details – she had just explained where babies came from.

This became part of my social education, but I realized that facts alone were not enough. I would have to work on my self-confidence. Up to now, it had been very difficult for me to venture out in public by myself. I decided that I would have to stop relying so much on other people and start doing things on my own.

So I found a ritzy bar that was close to the school (people in Europe can get into bars at an earlier age). It opened in late afternoon but was usually pretty empty until evening. I took a deep breath and walked in. The bartender was stocking bottles on the shelves in preparation for the evening. He smiled at me as I sat down and ordered an orange juice.

My heart was beating so loudly, I was sure he could hear it. I fought the impulse to flee and forced myself to stay seated. Even if the friendly bartender couldn't hear my heart, surely my insecurity was apparent. He brought me a bowl of peanuts and talked with me for a while. Eventually, I became more relaxed and the next visit was easier. For several weeks, I frequented the bar, practising my social skills until all the fear was gone. Looking back, I'm especially grateful that the people I met during this time were so friendly and helpful. It kept me safe for a long time before trouble finally found me.

Beloved Sabine,

So much has changed here about the house. One can't even compare it to our old hut at the Klihi River. I even have a real wood oven and can now bake bread. Papa installed some solar panels on the roof, so we have some electrical light. (But we can barely use it because it attracts so many insects into the house.)

I think a lot about the past. We all miss you. The Fayu constantly ask how you are doing and when you're coming back. Fusai recently brought us a large piece of sago and told me how much you used to like sago – especially with living worms in it. Your father still sits around the campfire every evening, talking to the Fayu. Sometimes they tell each other stories about all the mischief you got into as a kid. I can always tell when they're talking about you because of their loud laughter.

Your father also said recently how much he misses you kids and that it isn't as nice as in the old days when you were still here. Oh Sabine, I hope that you don't forget your time in the jungle and that you always know how important you are in our life. 'The salt in the soup' is how I describe you. I simply can't imagine a life without you. Please don't forget us, because we all love you very much.

As I read this poignant letter from my mother, I felt again the odd pain that had been increasing in recent days. More and more often, the jungle would come to mind, especially as I lay in bed at night. But I repressed the thoughts and feelings, whose only goal, it seemed, was to make me cry. No! I was here now and would become like those around me. That is my goal, isn't it? After all, wasn't I a European now? I put the letter away and tried not to think about it.

A few weeks later, I got my first boyfriend. He was a model – very attractive and well-built. We met shooting pool, and I immediately fell in love, as he was the most handsome man I had ever seen. On our second date, he asked if I wanted to sleep with him. I was a little confused. Was that normal practice? I had the courage to tell him that it was too early for me. Over the next several weeks, we met as often as possible for hiking trips and endless conversations. I was so in love that I called my grandmother and told her that I was going to marry this man.

He told me about his dream of becoming an actor. But most of all, he told me that I should sleep with him. After all, he loved me and wanted to show me. And I was fresh from the jungle and extremely naïve. So one day, he got what he wanted.

Back at school, I proudly told Leslie that I was no longer a virgin. But she didn't react the way I expected. Instead, she got angry and told me that she thought it was a pity that I hadn't waited for the right one.

'But I did!' I said, not understanding her disapproval. And that was the end of that conversation.

A few days later, a classmate came up to me and said that my boyfriend was married and had a child. I was so shocked that I didn't believe a single word. No! Impossible! This man couldn't have lied, couldn't have been unfaithful. I ran into the house and got into the shower, the only place where you could have some privacy. And then the tears started. I cried so hard I couldn't stand up any more. I collapsed on the floor of the shower and stuffed a washcloth in my mouth to mute my screaming. *What have I done?* I thought over and over. *What have I done?*

Was I now damned? He must be my man – he had slept with me. That's how it was in the world in which I had grown up. I didn't understand anything any more. I sat there in the shower, feeling more lost than ever.

For the first time in my young life, I truly experienced abject terror. But I didn't really know what I was afraid of. It occurred to me in this moment that the perfect modern world we children had discussed in the jungle was only a figment of our imaginations. The world in which I found myself was a completely foreign one and always would be. I felt caught but would only understand much later how true that was. I was caught between two worlds, in the clutches of a fantasy that was never going to be true.

Eight years later, I was on the way to a doctor's appointment in Vevey when I met the man again. Over coffee, he told me that he was divorced now and still wanted to become an actor. To my surprise, he also apologized to me. 'I forgave you a long time ago,' I answered. 'I learned a lot through my experience with you.' That was the last time I saw him.

I eventually climbed out of the shower, and life moved on. Leslie and Susanne left school, and a new school year began. I was very sad to lose my friend and 'life consultant', but I did make friends with three new students from Japan, England and Denmark. We had an exciting year together.

I had adapted fairly well by then, although appearances can be deceiving. It was a sheltered life at the Château Beau Cèdre, a life in a golden cage. We were treated as adults in some ways, for which I was thankful. Those like me, who were over eighteen, were allowed to leave for the weekend. But in general, it was a fairly structured environment. We followed a strict schedule and always knew what we had to do next.

And so the second year went by, and I increasingly suppressed the memory of home. I lived almost on automatic pilot. I only felt the pain deep inside myself when I received letters from Mama. Otherwise, I kept myself too busy to notice it.

Then one afternoon, I got a short letter from Papa.

My dear daughter,

Almost every evening we sit around the fire in front of the house – it really is a wonderful view – and the Fayu speak about you. They remember when you ate crocodile and wild boar with them. They really want to see you again. Tuare keeps asking when you will finally return to your Fayu brother. I tried to explain to him that you are very far away. 'When the sun goes down here,' I told him, 'it goes up where Sabine is. And when she eats her sago, we are sleeping.'

As I read this, I suddenly felt extremely homesick. I went to my room and cried. My carefully built façade of a modern young woman began to crumble. The jungle child could no longer be ignored. For the first time since my arrival, I had the clear thought *I need to go back soon, very soon.* It wasn't long before my graduation, and so such a trip would fit readily into the schedule of my life.

But as so often happens, life had its own ideas. A dark period was ahead that I would just as soon forget. As sheltered as my life had been up to that point, I was about to be brutally thrown into the 'real' world – whether or not I was ready for it. It was to be a time during which I was completely alone and could depend only on myself. There would be no one to explain life's complexities and dangers, no one to take me by the hand to cross the street. I would feel utterly helpless and alone during the darkest chapter of my life.

44

ALONE

Dear Sabine,

Thank you for the wonderful pictures. What can I say? I look at them every day. Baby Sophia – I can hardly believe it. I hung a couple of the photos on the wall. My favourite is the one where she is lying in the basket and looks so yellow. I can barely wait to meet her.

We showed the Fayu the pictures of Sophia. They were wild with excitement when they heard it was your baby. Fusai asked if a man had 'stolen' you. I told her yes, that you were stolen in the true sense, and that the man didn't even ask us. Fusai found this unacceptable.

Nakire's first reaction was, 'Now I am a grandfather.'

'How's that?' Papa asked. 'I'm the grandfather, not you.'

'But so am I,' Nakire responded. 'Sabine is my daughter as well.' On that they could agree. Nakire grinned from ear to ear. He thinks you should come back soon – after all, he wants to see 'his' granddaughter.

I had met another young man and found myself pregnant shortly after graduation. (Leslie had forgotten to tell me that condoms don't always work.) I went to Germany for the delivery, and when Sophia arrived, I had no idea what to do. Finally, I returned to Switzerland and married the father of my child. A year later, I became pregnant again and had a son, Lawrence. My husband and I divorced not long after.

I felt like I was sinking in quicksand and couldn't breathe. It was as though I was being pulled down into a vortex of oppression and couldn't get out. Homesickness for the jungle plagued me every day. The nightmares returned.

The only spot of joy was my children. I loved them more than anything, but they were also the reason I couldn't return to the jungle. I didn't want to leave them behind, but I couldn't take them with me to Indonesia. So I stayed in Switzerland, pursued my education further, and began working.

I tried to present a perfect façade but on the inside felt only fear, desperation and the sense that I wasn't enough – that something was lacking in me. I stopped speaking about my childhood and where my roots were.

I went through life as if I were in a dream, and I tried to fit in. But that only made things worse. I kept sinking. Everything in my life seemed to go wrong. I no longer knew friend from foe. Nothing was clear to me. Instead of black and white, there was only grey.

As time passed, I increasingly felt as though I was sitting in a small boat in the middle of the ocean, without sail, paddle or rudder. A mighty storm raged above my head – a malevolent darkness that swirled around me. Lightning, thunder and huge waves crashed over me again and again. I had lost all control and desperately clung to the boat. When each new wave hit, I wondered whether it would be the end of me. And I couldn't seem to get my footing again before another wave came and threw me down. My screams for help went unheard because in my fear, I had become mute.

I had lost everything. My house, my family, my dreams, my joy. Everything was gone. I fought alone in a world that was still foreign to me and whose rules and customs I simply couldn't master. My parents were in the jungle, my siblings in America. It felt as though someone had forcibly ripped me from my family, and yet a single phone call from me would have been enough to reestablish contact with them. So why didn't I make that call? I'm not sure. I was probably still suffering from profound culture shock – something I didn't recognize until much later. I couldn't think clearly and didn't seem to have the strength to be proactive. I didn't know what was happening to me.

And then, at my lowest point, I lost my job. Now I really had nothing. Not even food in the fridge. I came home late one day after having dropped off my kids at their father's house, and as I stepped into my cold, dark apartment, I simply came undone. I collapsed on the floor and started crying. My thoughts were fuzzy and scattered. I wanted to rip out the pain inside me. I didn't want to live any more.

And then I did something I never thought I'd do. The memory of it haunts me still. I crawled into the bathroom and pulled the blade from a razor. The cool metal between my fingers felt good. I was overwhelmed by the thought of being able to cut out the pain. Out of my mind, I drew the blade across my skin and felt a short, stabbing pain. Then I sat and watched the drops of blood run down my arm.

Suddenly, I felt relief. It was wonderful how the physical pain was able to distract me from the emotional pain. In a daze, I cut myself again and again. First one wrist, then the other. I cut deeper and deeper and had the feeling that I could somehow save everything this way – my children, my family, my life.

But then I glanced in the mirror and was shocked to the core. A ghost looked back at me, chalky white. Black mascara was smeared over my entire face. Dazed, confused eyes.

Then reality slapped me in the face. I dropped the razor blade and looked around. My arms, the floor, my clothing – everything was covered in blood. I started to scream. I stuffed my hand in my mouth but couldn't stifle the sound. I sat on the cold floor until the screaming turned into whimpering. Lethargy spread over me; I just wanted to lie down and close my eyes.

I looked up wearily and realized that I was still bleeding. Everything was red and in a perverse way was quite pretty. In the blood that ran from my body, I could see the pain flowing out, too. As my life ended, so would my pain.

And then, as if in final farewell, I prayed for the first time in a very long time. It was the prayer that had escorted me throughout my childhood.

> He who dwells in the shelter of the Most High
> will rest in the shadow of the Almighty. I will say of
> the Lord, 'He is my refuge and my fortress, my
> God, in whom I trust . . .'
> . . . no harm will befall you, no disaster will come
> near your tent. For he will command his angels
> concerning you to guard you in all your ways.
> —Psalm 91: 1–2, 10–11

Oh God, what have I done? rang through my head. I was suddenly wide awake. I grabbed two towels and wrapped them tightly around my wrists. Everything hurt, and the bleeding didn't want to stop. I pressed harder against my wounds. When the bleeding stopped, I leaned against the wall and closed my eyes. The bloody towels remained around my wrists.

I thought back over my life. Everything I had seen and experienced played like a movie across my mind: Nepal, the mountains, the stars, the jungle, the Fayu, Tuare, the Sunday River, the wars, the hate, the love, Ohri's death, my parents and finally my children. I saw the joy and the pain. I thought about my life with the Fayu and here in Europe. Most of all, I thought about my parents, who had taught me the meaning of love, and about my beloved children.

Suddenly, I viewed myself with astonishment. Hadn't I learned to survive in a jungle? Hadn't I managed to bridge the gap between the Stone Age and the modern age in a matter of a few brief years? What had happened to my strength? Where were my will to survive and my joy over living? Where was the true me? Surely I could learn to be happy in the civilized world – after all, it was simply another kind of jungle.

Please God, help me, I whispered. *I can't do this any more.* I let my head sink to the ground and fell asleep. That night I had another dream of Ohri. But this time there was no burning hut, no young man begging for help. I dreamed I was in the jungle again, sitting on the log in front of our house, admiring the beauty of the jungle. Suddenly Ohri appeared in front of me, big and strong, with a warm smile. He sat down next to me, took my hand, and said only one sentence: 'I never left you.'

When I woke up the next morning, I had an inner peace

I had not felt for a long time. I got up and cleaned the dried blood away. I bandaged my wrists, changed clothes and lay down in bed. Tears began to flow again, but this time they were tears of relief and not desperation. I had come to a decision – I would fight. As I had in the jungle, I would learn to survive here, becoming strong enough again that I could return home. The path before me was not an easy one, but it would lead to happiness. I wanted to wake up in the morning and find joy in life.

And so I began to fight for my heart – with the goal to make proactive decisions that would get my life back on track. While I'm still fighting the good fight to this day, I have managed to regain my courage and strength. I have built a new life and learned that happiness doesn't come from external things but from places inside my own heart. The journey continues toward finding my true self, the meaning of my life, and the place where I belong. Whether in the jungle or the western world, I am determined to find my happiness and joy.

45

FULL CIRCLE BACK TO THE BEGINNING

Many years have passed since the day I decided to take control of my life again. After a lengthy time in Switzerland and a briefer time in Japan, I moved back to Germany two years ago. During years of travelling, I have reinvented myself several times over.

I recently went to get my national identification papers. The government official gave me the relevant forms. But even after I signed them, she kept looking at me expectantly. When I didn't react, she informed me that I had to surrender my old identification papers before she could issue new ones.

Oh no, I thought. *Not again!* Taking a deep breath, I explained to her as I had a hundred times before to a hundred other government officials that I didn't have old papers to give her. I had neither been born nor had I grown up in Germany. And after a bit of a delay, she finally gave me my first German identification card. I was thirty-one.

When I moved to Germany this last time, I integrated

myself into society without feeling like a foreigner. I bought a car, rented an apartment, and began to fight my way through the substantial German bureaucracy. Health insurance, life insurance, retirement programs, rental agreements, tax numbers, cable television. Register here, unregister there, this document, that form – it seemed to never end. All of this was a new experience for me, but I managed. And today I live in a small town, determined to find happiness here.

It is a real advantage to have grown up in the Fayu culture. They occasionally still ask my father, 'How is Sabine? Is her heart happy?' They don't ask how big my house is or how many wild boars I own. Their concern for me has nothing to do with my social standing. As long as I manage to keep in mind the lessons of the jungle, life goes well. I learned there that one should enjoy the simple things in life. That life is not defined by the things you own but rather by the way you spend your time. I learned from the Fayu that happiness comes from contentment rather than acquisition. And for these lessons, I am grateful.

But it was only when I began writing my story that something changed in me. It was like waking up from a long dream. For the first time in years, I began to understand myself, why I reacted in the ways I did or why I made certain decisions. And for the first time, I began to really feel again, allowing these memories of my life to surface. Over the last several months, I have relived my childhood. I have laughed and cried. In my mind's eye, I have watched the sunrises again and crossed the river by canoe, enjoying the nature around me. I have gone through photographs and old home movies, read my diaries, and reminisced with my family.

And now that I have reached the end of this book, I've

come to the realization that I need to go back to my home in the jungle. When I left the tribe fifteen years ago, I left with the intention of returning soon, but I never returned, not even for a visit. I became trapped in this world, moving from one place to another, always with the feeling that I was in the wrong place. I realize now that I never had the chance to say good-bye.

I have also learned that the definition of home is not necessarily a country, state or town or even a certain culture. Home is where the heart is, surrounded by the ones we love and who love us.

But most important of all, I came to understand that I belong to two worlds and two cultures at the same time. And although a part of me has become western, having adapted to the life and culture here, a part of me is and will always remain a jungle child.

Dear Sabine,

This letter your dear old Papa is writing to you is bound up in great sorrow. Chief Baou has died.

I had been told over the radio recently that Chief Baou was deathly ill. I immediately made plans to visit him, but by the time I arrived in the village, he was all ready dead. I cried many tears of sorrow. Then Nakire came to me and told me the following story:

A few days before his death, Chief Baou got scared. He knew his time was running out, so he called a trusted friend. For three days, he confessed his sins – every man, woman and child he had murdered. As you know, Sabine, he had been a brutal warrior in his day.

At the end of his confessions, peace came into his heart. When the Fayu who had assembled around his hut began to cry, he said to them, 'Why are you crying?

You should be happy for me. Because now I will get to see Afou guti (the Great Father).'

'Hold on Chief Baou. Klausu will be here soon,' Nakire said. He knew that I had just landed in Kordesi. But Chief Baou said, 'Why should I wait for Klausu? I all ready know him. I'd rather see Afou guti.' One by one he said good-bye to those present, laid his head back, and died. I'm told that he looked very peaceful. Finally, right before his death, he found the peace he'd been looking for his whole life.

And Sabine, I pray that you will one day find the peace and joy that you are looking for. I'm thinking of you and hugging you tightly . . .

Your Papa.

EPILOGUE

We recently held our first family reunion in ten years in Germany. Judith and Christian both came from America, where they live with their spouses. Papa had recently returned from the jungle, and Mama had all ready been in Germany a while.

We sat around the dining table and discussed my plans for the book. From outside, we could hear my children and Judith's son excitedly speaking in a conglomeration of German, English and French.

Mama sighed. 'Having your children around brings back a lot of memories. When you three were young, nobody could understand you unless they could speak English, German and Indonesian.'

'What do you mean, "when we were young"?' Christian raised his eyebrows in amusement. 'We still talk that way when we're together. And Papa is the worst one of all.'

'I remember the first letter I got from Papa after going to England,' giggled my very pregnant sister as she helped herself to a piece of chocolate cake. 'I laughed for days – it was written in at least four languages. That you're planning to write an entire book only in German is remarkable, Sabine. I don't think I could do that any more.'

'Well, we all know that when Sabine sets her mind to something, she gets it done no matter what stands in her way,' Papa said with a grin.

'Are you going to tell the story about how you threw the dead snake around my neck?' Judith asked.

'And what about the time you took the chewing gum from Germany and wrapped it around your head?' Christian added.

'That's right! And I had to cut off all your hair,' Mama laughed.

'But you have the best story, Mama. Do you remember when you dumped the bucket of water on top of the warrior's head?' I snorted.

'And then gave him my only towel!' Papa added with amused indignation.

Mama asked, 'Did I ever tell you the story of how I gave Papa the shock of his life? All the Fayu had gone down the hill, and the village was empty, which Papa didn't know. I saw Papa coming up the hill, so I quickly took off all my clothes. When he arrived at the house, I stood outside on the porch, calmly eating some sago. If Papa had had false teeth, they would have fallen out in moral protest. I almost fell down laughing.'

'Oh yeah, and do you remember when . . .'

For a long time, we sat together as a family and reminisced about the beauty, the sadness, the tragic and the comic things we had experienced. Sometimes we laughed until tears came into our eyes; other times we sat quietly and remembered our Fayu friends who had died.

Life in the jungle has marked us all. We are each grateful and feel truly gifted to have had such an unusual and wonderful life. And we are deeply indebted to the Fayu who shared their lives with us and accepted us as part of their tribe despite our different skin colour and culture. They deserve our highest gratitude.

The work with the Fayu continues until today. The organization my parents work for, YPPM, has taken over a large part of the developmental aid efforts – in particular, the school that my mother founded, where members of the younger generation learn to read, write, do maths and speak Indonesian. (It is an Indonesian law that all citizens must learn the Indonesian language.)

The Fayu have become a peaceful tribe, in stark contrast to when we first joined them. The population is growing, and the infant mortality rate has been dramatically lowered. Life expectancy has risen from thirty-five years at the time of our arrival to fifty years. Through their own strength and courage, the Fayu have made significant steps forward.

What especially pleases us is that they are now better prepared to protect their tribe and land from those who might try to take it from them. This has included helping them understand that they shouldn't trust every promise that is made by outsiders. We have tried to teach them that their land is valuable and that they have rights within Indonesian society. The local government is very supportive of our efforts. A delegation recently visited the Fayu – a great honour for all of us.

And despite or maybe because of all these changes, my parents continue to work tirelessly to preserve the original and unique culture of the Fayu. They encourage them to continue their craftsmanship of bows, arrows, stone axes and nets. And my parents have emphasized the importance of passing on the stories of the past, the claim to their land,

and the lessons of survival to the next generation. If the elders don't pass along what they know, the culture will be lost.

The Fayu truly are an unusual and special nation. They can be proud of their heritage and the fact that against all odds, they have become a vibrant people once again.

ACKNOWLEDGEMENTS

First of all, I want to thank my business partner, Britta Marks, who convinced me to write this book, supported me in the process and taught me to be proud of my childhood.

Thanks go to my agent, Lionel von dem Knesebeck, for paving the way for this book's existence.

Thanks also to Droemer Knaur Verlag, especially Dr. Hans-Peter Übleis, who believed in this book from the very beginning, and to my editor, Carolin Graehl. She graciously made something readable out of my English-German grammar while still maintaining my style. My appreciation to Susanne Klein, who dedicated her energy to this book; Klaus Kluge, who listened to my opinions about marketing strategy with patience and (usually) a smile; Dominik Huber for the fantastic website; and all the others who accepted me with friendliness, lent me their computers, and provided me with coffee and sweets (thanks, Barbara!).

Thanks also to Birgit Matthies and Ariungerel 'Agi' Batdelger, who lovingly cared for my children, providing me the time to write this book.

To my family, Klaus-Peter, Doris and Christian Kuegler – heartfelt thanks for reminding me of the details of my childhood. Most of all, I want to thank my sister, Judith Kuegler Webster, who travelled from the United States while pregnant to help me write the book.

And last but not least, I want to thank the readers. I hope that this book has enriched your life a little and given you insight into a different world.

Appendix A

SOME INTERESTING FACTS ABOUT IRIAN JAYA

Irian Jaya is the western half of the world's third-largest island (behind Australia and Greenland). The eastern half of the island is the independent nation of Papua New Guinea (PNG). Irian Jaya (recently renamed West Papua) is Indonesia's largest and easternmost province.

The People:

- The population of West Papua is estimated at approximately 1,800,000.
- The indigenous people of Irian Jaya are distinguished into about 250 subgroups. This grouping is based on physical features and differences in language, customs, artistic expression and other aspects of culture.
- There are at least 250 major languages spoken by the indigenous people. The language and subgroup count has been hampered by the isolated nature of such tribes as the Fayu and so may still be an underestimation of the diversity on this island. The current count of 250

languages means that Irian Jaya contains one-fourth of the world's known languages (800), as well as numerous dialects.

Natural Wonders:
- Irian Jaya contains the world's deepest natural harbour (Humboldt Harbour, Jayapura).
- It has the only permanent glacier of any tropical Island. Its 'wintry' heritage also includes snowcapped mountain peaks that tower 5,000 metres over glacial lakes.
- It has the second-largest single tract of rain forest in the world (after the Amazon). The jungles of Irian Jaya are some of the most impenetrable in the world.
- Irian Jaya is famous for its bird of paradise. Of the forty-three species of this bird, thirty-five are found only on the island of West Papua/Papua New Guinea. Some of the indigenous tribes use bird of paradise plumes in their dress and rituals, a trend that was echoed in European ladies' fashions. Hunting for plumes and habitat destruction due to deforestation has resulted in some species being driven to endangered status.
- Lake Sentani is now freshwater but was once saltwater. Consequently, at one time, you used to be able to catch freshwater swordfish and sharks there.

History

In 1883, the island of New Guinea was split into three portions. The Dutch claimed the western half, while the eastern half became German New Guinea in the north and British Papua in the south. The Dutch began serious exploration in about 1898.

Serious disagreement between the Netherlands and Indonesia over ownership of Irian Jaya persisted until the

Dutch gave up the colony in 1963. Although Indonesia gained independence from the Netherlands in 1949, Indonesia did not gain claim to Irian Jaya until a UN-sponsored referendum in 1969.

General Douglas MacArthur used Sentani as a headquarters during the island campaigns of World War II. Evidence of this remains, as an area of the city is still called Camp K, and a popular local beach goes by the name Base G. Several of General MacArthur's machine-gun emplacements are still in position on the island.

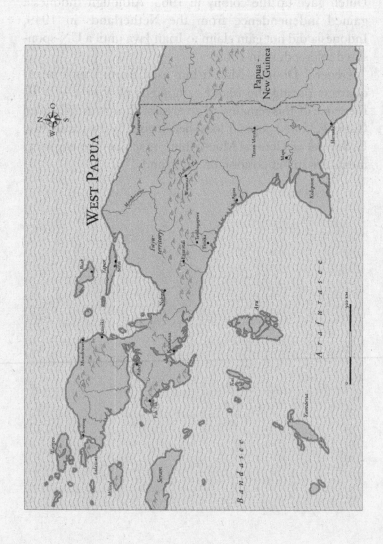

Appendix B

PEOPLE, PLACES, ANIMALS AND LANGUAGE

People
The Kuegler family includes parents Klaus and Doris (also called Klausu and Doriso) and children Judith, Sabine and Christian (also called Babu).

Nepali People
Danuwar Rai: The Nepalese tribe with whom the Kuegler family lived

Jungle Tribes of Indonesia
Dani, Bauzi, Dou, Kirikiri, Doa and Fayu. The Fayu are subdivided into four clans: the Iyarike, Tigre, Tearue and Sefoidi.

The Fayu
Chief Baou: Tigre chieftain and most respected chief among all the Fayu clans
Biya: The first Fayu woman whom Doris helped in

childbirth. Her little girl was named Doriso Bosa (Little Doris) and later became Tuare's wife.

Dawai: Nakire's first wife

Diro: He and his two brothers were orphaned when Chief Baou killed their parents. Diro later became the best friend of and advisor to Chief Baou's son, Isori.

Fusai: Nakire's second wife and the daughter of a Tigre chieftain

Chief Kologwoi: Iyarike chieftain

Nakire: The young Iyarike man who grew up among the Dou and became Klaus's expedition guide. Nakire served as Klaus's translator and advisor on matters of Fayu culture.

Ohri: An orphaned Fayu child who became like a part of the Kuegler family

Teau: Iyarike war chief

Tuare, Bebe, Dihida, Abusai, Ohri, Ailakokeri and Isori: Fayu children who served as Sabine and Christian's primary playmates

Ziau: A Fayu chieftain

Other People

Herb: An American researcher who accompanied Klaus on his expeditions to locate the Fayu

John: An American developer who had an unexpected encounter with some Fayu while he was surveying Kordesi before building the landing strip

Minius: A Dani orphan who was taken in by the Kueglers and who, as an adult, worked for them

Rex: An American pilot

Places

Danau Bira: A base camp in the middle of the jungle of Irian Jaya

Foida: The Fayu village in which the Kuegler family built their house

Irian Jaya: The western half of the island that contains Papua New Guinea. Irian Jaya belongs to Indonesia.

Jayapura: The coastal city in Indonesia in which the Kuegler family first lived before going to the jungle

Klihi River: Main river running through Fayu territory

Kordesi: The Dou village halfway between Foida and Danau Bira and the site of a landing strip for small planes

Patan: A suburb of Kathmandu, Nepal, where Sabine and Christian were born

Polita: A Dou village near Kordesi

Sabine's Animals

Timmy (cat), George (mouse), Bobby (parrot), Daddy Longlegs (spider), Hanni and Nanni (ostriches), Jumper (tree kangaroo), Wooly (cuscus)

Language

Afou (Fayu: dad)

asahaego (Fayu: could mean 'good morning', 'good night', 'thank you', 'good-bye' and more)

awaru kaha (Fayu: could mean 'I am doing well', 'I am happy' or 'I am a good person and haven't done anything wrong')

bagai (Fayu: arrow made of bamboo used to hunt wild pigs and ostriches)

Bau (Fayu: yes)

di (Fayu: depending on pitch, can mean 'water,' 'knife' or 'boar')

fai (Fayu: an arrow made from kangaroo bone that is designed to kill people)

fay (Fayu: bad)

Fu (Fayu: depending on pitch, can mean either 'log' or 'canoe')

hau (Fayu: no)

Kaha (Fayu: good)

kasbi (Fayu: a tree root that tastes like potato)

Kui (Fayu: depending on pitch, can mean either message or grand-father)

kwa (Fayu: breadfruit)

parang (Indonesian: a long machete)

sago (Fayu: a breadlike food made from the heart of the swamp palm)

zehai (Fayu: wood-tipped arrow used for hunting small animals and birds)

MARRIED TO A BEDOUIN

Marguerite van Geldermalsen

'"Where you staying?" the Bedouin asked. "Why you not stay with me tonight – in my cave?" He seemed enthusiastic – and we were looking for adventure.'

Thus begins Marguerite van Geldermalsen's story of how a New Zealand-born nurse became the wife of Mohammad Abdallah Othman, a Bedouin souvenir-seller from the ancient city of Petra in Jordan. It was 1978 and she and a friend were travelling through the Middle East when Marguerite met the charismatic Mohammad and decided that he was the man for her. Their home was lofty two-thousand-year-old cave carved into the red rock of a hillside. She became the resident nurse and learned to live like the Bedouin: cooking over fires, hauling water on donkeys and drinking sweet black tea, and over the years she became s much of a curiosity as the cave-dwellers with tourists such as Mary Lovell and Frank McCourt encouraging her to tell this, her extraordinary story.

DESERT DAWN

Waris Dirie

Fashion model, UN ambassador and courageous spirit, Waris Dirie is a remarkable woman, born into a family of tribal desert nomads in Somalia. She told her story – enduring female circumcision at five years old; running away at twelve through the desert to escape an arranged marriage; being discovered as she worked as a cleaner in London; and becoming a top fashion model – in her book, the worldwide bestseller, *Dersert Flower*.

although Waris Dirie fled Somalia, she never forgot the country that moulded her. She traces the roots of her courage, resilience and humour back to her culture, and most particularly to her mother.

This is the moving story of her return to Somalia – *Desert Dawn* is about coming home.

'I wanted to return to the place where I was born and see it with new eyes. I had no idea where my family was in Somalia. At first it seemed impossible – almost as impossible as a camel girl becoming a fashion model . . .'

DESERT FLOWER

Waris Dirie

'A story that traverses continents, spans worlds of
human experience and human pain . . . Waris Dirie was a
victim once, but she never will be again. She is still fighting,
still using her beauty and courage to take what
she has learned to try and put things right'
Sunday Express

'She was circumcised at five, fled an arranged marriage at
twelve, then became a Pirelli girl in her teens. Now,
Waris Dirie is an ambassador for the UN'
Observer

'Born a Somalian nomad, by the time she made it as a top
model, she'd survived genital mutilation and face-off
with a tiger . . .She's now a UN special Ambassador.
Take a cue from Waris's charm and courage'
Company

'Her first job was for a Pirelli calendar shoot – with Terence
Donovan – along with a young unknown girl from Streatham
called Naomi Campbell . . . Now author of a book, published
in 14 languages, which has had such a powerful effect
on Elton John that he has bought the movie rights'
Company

virago

To buy any of our books and to find out more
about Virago Press and Virago Modern Classics,
our authors and titles, as well as events and
book club forum, visit our websites

www.virago.co.uk
www.littlebrown.co.uk

and follow us on Twitter

@ViragoBooks

To order any Virago titles p & p free in the UK,
please contact our mail order supplier on:

+ 44 (0)1832 737525

Customers not based in the UK should contact
the same number for appropriate postage
and packing costs.